Praise for *Are We Home Yet?*

"Through her brilliant writing Katy somehow manages to put you right beside her in the scenes that make up her fascinating life. Funny, pin-sharp and wise, Katy's writing gets under your skin and right into your heart."

—Kit de Waal, author of
Supporting Cast and *My Name Is Leon*,

"What I love about Katy's writing is her diligence to emotional clarity, and her ability to find the humour in what to many of us would feel tragic. She balances personal experience with a wry sensibility so that what she has to say feels vital, and especially about the complexities of 21st century working-class women. It's about time her voice was heard."

—Lisa Blower, author of
Pondweed and *It's Gone Dark Over Bill's Mother's*

"Katy's writing is unflinchingly honest and undeniably authentic. It is also funny, sharp and full of perfectly placed detail. She challenges our preconceptions whilst transporting us right into the middle of a world few of us have had a chance to see this clearly before."

—Sharon Duggal, author of
Should ~~We Be~~ Behind and *The Handsworth Times*

fascinating given that Katy herself doesn't see it as 'over-coming' at all, rather her childhood 'constructed' her. I love this sentiment."

—Bookish Chat

"Half the pieces are by unpublished writers.... they are all sharp and bright."

—Robert Colls, *Literary Review*

Are We Home Yet?

Katy Massey

JACARANDA

TWENTY in 2020
Black Writers, British Voices

This edition first published in Great Britain 2020
Jacaranda Books Art Music Ltd
27 Old Gloucester Street,
London WC1N 3AX
www.jacarandabooksartmusic.co.uk

A CIP catalogue record for this book is available from the
British Library

ISBN: 9781913090197
eISBN: 9781913090395

Cover Design: Rodney Dive
Typeset by: Kamillah Brandes

Printed and bound by CPI Group (UK) Ltd, Croydon, CR0 4YY

To all my families, born, made and chosen.
And especially for Mam, who made me who I am.

1.

This Book Begins Like This

In the dream I am waiting in a room and I look around. I recognise the matching polished pine G-Plan dining table at which I sit, the deep-orange shaggy rug is cosily familiar beneath my feet. This is 24 Victoria Park Avenue, the house where I grew up. The nearest thing I had to a home during the closest experience I had to a childhood.

A couple of feet behind my chair the orange rug gives away gradually to stony moss and miniature ferns. The roots of trees rear up around the table, a green guard for the brown-and-orange dining arrangement. In the background I can hear birds' wings catch branches, causing dappled light streaming through the leaf canopy to dance on the G-plan table's mirror-like surface. A verdant discothèque, the light falls now on teacups of finest china and gold-leaf, then on glittering plates which shine like huge gold coins and are piled high with French fancies and Battenberg cake.

I am waiting at this table. I wait in a state of long-term expectation, where all tensions are balanced so perfectly that I appear to be calm. It is the epic wait of

Miss Haversham at her wedding breakfast. I appear to have mastered acceptance but instead have achieved a state of constant, considered anticipation. In exact opposition to the way that one usually 'just knows' in dreams, I do not know why I am waiting. I am not waiting for guests: they are already here. They surround me and all the chairs that usually remain empty are, in this imaginary time, filled.

My brother Paul is sat at the table, grinning so wide his face is split like a custard cream. I am angry with Paul—will I ever stop being angry with Paul?—but I am so happy to see him I grin through the tension. I wonder if he is convinced by my dream-smile. My Daddy is there too. Or rather Cyril? Or Father? No, I never had the chance to grow out of calling him Daddy, so I stick with it. It is the right decision, because he is smiling back at me and calling me his Khaki Princess, like he did before. I am looking at him hard but I can't make out his features. But I know it is him because I can see the outline of the hat he always wore, like someone just stepped off the boat.

Mam is at the tea-party as well—for a tea-party it is—and everyone is tucking into the fine china tea and colourful cake except me. I'm the only one who is looking on, observing. I am the only one who is confused. Beneath the noise of raised voices, laughs and chinking cups I am muttering that this can't be real, not even dream-real. Mam glances at me with a look that belongs to the time when I was little. Her eyes say 'are you ok' and also 'you'll feel the back of my hand if you don't behave'. But the look lasts only an instant— too quick for me to ask what she and the others are doing here. And anyway, how did she become so young?

Her hair is dye-it-yourself red and piled up on top of her head, her figure rounded but firm and her face open and almost unlined by time. She has turned her attention to my brother Andrew, who looks to be about 18, is wearing the long brown leather duster coat he is clearly very proud of. He is laughing too and my memory is snagged by the blueness of his eyes.

I know it is all wrong. Mam's tight-fitting dress that she hasn't worn since 1979, Daddy's out-of-focus features, Paul's brilliant laughter and Andrew's garrulous eyes. It is not that some of these people are dead, nor that in life they were never all together, never mind enjoyed tea parties. It is not even that I am the only one who has aged. I should be about ten years old, but I am almost thirty years older and appear to be the only one around this table who is not fixed in time, stuck at this party among the trees and the birds, where the tea and cake will never run out and conversation comes as easy as breath.

No, what is wrong is that I am the only one waiting: suspended between what has been and what could be, suspended in the realm of the possible for as long as I manage not to breathe out. I am sitting in the bosom of my fractured, half-dead family holding my breath for dear life, and I am waiting to go home.

2.

Long Division

It's a chilly spring day, three decades before the dream, and so far it is like any other weekday afternoon. I am ten years old, or perhaps eleven, and we two girls dawdle hand in hand on the way home from school, kicking stones and giggling in the remains of the late afternoon sun. The cracked concrete pavement takes us past rows and rows of suburban red-brick semis and tarmac drives. There are few trees, lots of hedges, green again now and alive with birds' nests. My friend Sarah is slim with peach-and-white skin and blonde bobbed hair. I am plump, with a halo of curly dark-brown hair shorn to about three inches long all around my large head. Sarah's pale white hand lies encased in my small brown one.

We have worked hard to wear our uniforms in a way that will mark us out as street-wise, even mildly rebellious. Our grey skirts are turned over at the waist so that the hem hovers a good three inches above our knees. The grubby collars of our regulation white shirts hold burgundy ties folded over and over into knots as fat as cravats. Our grey school jumpers are sometimes tied around our waists but today are draped around our necks like scarves. The hated St Benedict's burgundy boiled-wool blazers are slung over our bags, so we shiver in the late spring wind and chat through jaws clenched to stop our teeth chattering. Hidden under my white shirt, around my neck is a Yale key suspended from a grey piece of string. It bounces comfortably against my chest's turgid brown flesh as we walk.

"Did you see Jane Brennan's face when Gerry Ward said he fancied Sam Reeves?" Sarah is full of who fancies whom in our class. Last Friday she even stayed late and snogged Ian Smith outside the fifth form entrance. I haven't been near a lad yet, but I am as intrigued as her.

"Jane's a cow anyway. And she wears Clark's shoes."

"Spastic-shoes! Sam wouldn't look at him anyway. She fancies Damon Hughes, but he's an altar boy."

"So what? They're the worst!"

Our throaty chuckles take us to the top of the Avenue where I live. We are nearly at my house, 24 Victoria Park Avenue, but our hands are still encased in each other, we are not willing to let go just yet.

"Come to my house and play. My Mam'll give you your tea," I say to Sarah, not really thinking what I'm saying. The atmosphere at my house has changed recently. Mam, who was always at work, is now always at home. There's no Daddy at home at the moment but there is more money for toys now. That's how I have my Girl's World doll's head, and how I know Mam won't mind giving Sarah her tea.

She thinks about this for a minute. "Can we play with your Girl's World?"

I eye my friend and realise, she looks a bit like the Girl's World, with her blue eyes and all that blonde hair. The Girl's World is ace. It is the toy everyone at school wants. Her hair is thick and luscious, and at a turn of a knob, her pony tail will grow out of the centre of her skull, like Rapunzel's hair. If you tip her head up, her eyes will flick from blue, to green, and eventually, to brown. She is perfect, she doesn't argue, she doesn't walk away, in fact she has no limbs. She is the perfect girl.

"OK, But I've bagged first play with the makeup. And I get to pull the hair out." My voice is firm. There will not be any more concessions.

"Alright, but I'll have to go home for my tea or my Mam'll go mad." Sarah concedes and the deal is done.

We have a plan that means the playing and giggling of the school day can go on and on, past *Blue Peter* and maybe even past *The News*. In excitement we run down the rest of the Avenue towards Number 24, keen to get out of the wind chapping our legs and the chill breathing goose-bumps over our arms. We climb the steps up to my old, glossy black front door, smooth and shiny from years of over-painting.

I bend over, fishing the Yale key from its home underneath my shirt and vest. I get hold of the string and pull at it, conjuring the still-warm brass from the top of my shirt collar. I bring it up to the lock, lifting first my neck, then my whole plump body up onto tiptoe, so that I can open the door without taking the key off. I turn the key and manage to open the front door a crack. Then I freeze.

Time slows down, and, though I don't know it yet, this is the moment I separate into two. The first version of me is a plump brown girl standing frozen to the spot, a piece of string stretching from her neck to the key still stuck in the door, swinging from the lock as if in a noose. With one foot inside the big black wooden door, I am listening carefully, head cocked toward the opening. There are odd and terrifying noises coming from inside my house.

My friend Sarah is stood close behind me, her blonde head trying to see past, to understand why our fun has come to a halt. Neither of us notices the second plump, brown girl, the same size but somehow less substantial, who has floated out of me, and is now bobbing above our heads, grey skirt fanned out like a parachute, navy knickers on display. She is calmly looking down on the unfolding scene. From now on, I will be two girls: an observant and secretive kid who is on the adolescent cusp of adulthood, and, at the same time, a noisy brown bundle of neurosis whose role is to protect the watchful, more vulnerable child.

I haven't yet realised that a part of me has gone, and Sarah hasn't noticed it either. I am still rooted to the spot—surely it has been hours now?—listening to the

16

sounds. It is a grunting, yowling noise. A woman's voice, but somehow distorted into a rhythmic crying-out I know I shouldn't be hearing. The sounds seem over-enthusiastic, and somehow deliberate like a bad actor repeating a mistake. The voice is high-pitched and coming from the front room.

I realise all at once two things: these are like the sounds a woman makes with pleasure and that is my Mam. I don't know how I know but I know it is Mam, making noises that I've heard from the television and the bits of films that make my brothers cough with embarrassment. Realising it, I do the only thing I can do and quickly pull the door closed. The lock reconnects and I fall back out of the porch and onto the doorstep. I have almost throttled myself in the process, and the scarlet in my cheeks is not purely due to embarrassment.

As I come apart from myself, Sarah peers closely at me and I stare back, stranded. I don't know if I have let the noise out, or if I managed to close the door quickly enough to keep it in. In the pause I am falling apart, literally becoming two people. I remain the plump playmate that Sarah takes me for, but I have also become someone else who floats just above us remaining watchful, alert.

This version of me knows that something has changed forever. That I cannot be the person I once was. Though I can pretend, that simple young girl has gone forever. It seems to take me a long time to get a grip on myself. Sarah senses that the thing that has just happened can't be talked about, she asks no questions and just stands there, embarrassed-looking, but still staring at me. This is just as well, because I can't think of a plausible excuse for shoving her backward out of the doorway.

"We'll have to go and play at your house," I eventually squeeze out, and Sarah wordlessly nods. She turns and leads the way to her house, where there won't be a Girl's World to play with but she can safely let us both into the warmth, and her Mam probably won't be home from work yet so we can drink milk and eat biscuits in front of children's telly. And anyway, her Mam almost certainly won't be having sex in the front room so Sarah's house can be home for today.

We are watched by the new, floating version of me while we entertain ourselves. We act as if nothing untoward happened at Victoria Park Avenue, playing with the new microwave oven in Sarah's kitchen and burning our lips and mouths on wet, rubbery slices of bread which we've heated until they gave off clouds of steam.

RentaGhost is on the telly and Sarah and I appear glued to the exploits of Claypole and Davenport. But the floating me needs to plan, she needs to get practical. As Sarah's laughter echoes around the room, I have time to think about the terrible noises I heard earlier. I can't tell Mam about them obviously, but how will I look at her, after this?

Most of all I am aware that something about me has permanently changed, but I am not quite sure what it is. I have to plan carefully, so I can guard Mam's secret without anyone knowing I am doing it, most of all her. I must have a laugh with my mates, pass my exams, and do all the usual things I like doing—like cooking potato waffles in the toaster but always guard Mam's secret. I am exhausted just thinking about it. But it seems the floating me knows something I don't. Because now that the decision for life-long secrecy is made and my plan has been hatched the phantom girl bobbing up near the living room pendant light begins to fade and slowly, slowly disappears.

3.

Landscapes

I am on the way to visit Mam for the evening, but I drive
to Leeds early and park the car at the station. I emerge
in front of the formerly blackened deco façade of The
Queens Hotel not quite knowing what to do with myself.
The trip was to see Mam, and my brother, and talk about
where Mam should live now she is older, lonely and in
need of more help. But, just for one afternoon, I wanted
to visit my hometown, feel like a native. I wanted to feel
welcome for a few hours in the city I used to call home,
so I drove into the town centre on a whim.

The hotel, like much of Leeds, had been renovated
since I ran around the centre as a teenager, buying under-
age drinks in Yates Wine Lodge and watching closing
time scuffles break out before boarding the last bus home.
Now, The Queens is proud and white, masking the ugly
station behind it. Standing there, wondering what to do
with this freedom I have handed myself, I notice that the
pristine paint on the hotel looks barely dry. I vacantly
stare at the office workers sitting in its shadow eating
lunchtime sandwiches among fuchsia-filled hanging

baskets and City Square's grumpy Victorian statuary.

I immediately feel out of place in this newly remade, optimistic City and realise that the journey is a mistake. I am still the girl I was, whereas Leeds is reborn out of its past. The industrial warehouses by the River Aire were still storage spaces then, now they are unsold apartments littering countless estate agents' windows. I walk through the oddly familiar streets, drawn to the key cutters, cobblers and fish and chip shops of my childhood, but I find my reminiscence is jostled by Starbucks and brand spanking shiny office blocks.

I am alone today and walking to retrace my teenage steps but, if I could, I would take you on a tour of this city and you could help me find the town centre I remember. From City Square we could walk together down Boar Lane, past the old Griffin Hotel. Before long, the unchanging red-brick glory of Kirkgate Market would bear down proudly on us. The Market is a constant. Of course, we will find it has changed too, but only to reflect the people who set up in business here and the shoppers that throng the halls. It has changed in the way that markets do, and shopping centres and shiny new office blocks don't.

I would quickly hustle you through the arched glass doors, thrilled to find a place which doesn't disappoint memory, and first I would show you the wrought iron clock that stands in monument to the retailing genius of Michael Marks. The clock is sited on the spot where

Marks' stall stood selling everything for a penny. Today, near the clock, we will browse a stall selling everything for a pound. Marks first pitched up in 1884, years before he met Tom Spencer and made history. But Leeds is not over-proud of him—after all he wasn't the first immigrant to end-up here, struggling to find a foothold in the city.

So we would be following Marks' ghost as I lead you through the maze of newer émigré stall-holders, past a whole row of butchers and into the high-smelling fish-market where we might buy dressed crabs and whelks. We would wander past the grinning faces of hopeful Asian proprietors gesturing to racks of ragtrade knock-offs, and we'd marvel at the speciality stalls dedicated to selling endless variations on a single item: Cheese, pork, day-old bread, sweeties already weighed out into four-ounce bags, bakery 'seconds', eggs, dried fruit, nuts, spices. We would see stalls for afro hair products, stalls for hair extensions, and stalls fashioned like shops, where you can go inside and visit a hairdresser.

You could get a Thai manicure, while I buy a cushion from the foamshop and overripe black-mottled plan-tain from the Jamaican grocers. We might notice that the Tripe Shop stands two units away from one selling 'Goods from Southern Africa'. By this time my sprits would be so lifted that I would turn to you with a chal-lenge: 'Tell me what you want and I will find it, for there is nothing alien here'.

If you were not exhausted by now and begging me to

let you rest your feet, and if you weren't bored stiff by my stories of the hours I spent here years ago, pocket-money tightly clutched in hand, looking for Constance Carroll cosmetics and fingerless gloves, we would continue our tour and walk up to the Town Hall and the civic centre of the City.

I would bid you gape at the Lions guarding the Town Halls' proud edifice and show you the wan Pre-Raphaelite heroines in the Art Gallery's collection of over-framed paintings. After this you would understand a little more of the city that made me, and we could board the bus for Kirkstall and trundle past Amen Corner and the old Truman Brewery on the River Aire, which, during the Eighties, belched out a dense savoury mist of hops and yeast. Eventually I'd ring the bell and we'd alight the bus opposite Binns' Newsagents and make our way up the hill toward Victoria Park Avenue and I would tell you stories of the motley crew it was home to.

And here I am, alone in front of the carcass of 24 Victoria Park Avenue. In the landscape of my memory, Number 24 occupies a site as close to a home as any. I spent perhaps only ten years in this house, off and on. But today, I need a focus for memories and this house frames them—even the memories of things which didn't happen there—because it was the place where our family life played out. In conversation I am often led back to it, because it was the only place where we were all together for any length of time. So finally, the force of resurgent memories has lead me back here in person, but I don't realise until I arrive and stand awkwardly in the quiet, week-day street that this place is obviously where I should have started this story.

I was not born here, I'm not even from Yorkshire. My Mam had upped sticks to Shropshire especially for that event. I rushed into the world during the last week of a hot July in the new town of Telford, Shropshire. My birth took place at home and my Mam was seen to by a midwife and some neighbours. Not so unusual in 1969, but it is a matter of family lore that one of these neighbours took my afterbirth home to burn in his incinerator. It was wrapped in newspaper but which one? Did it carry news of the moon landings a couple of days before? Or was it the local paper, full of letters complaining about Telford and Wrekin Council? Was that paper an augury, the first of greatness achieved, the second of an ordinary life, ordinarily lived? Anyway, at least half my afterbirth surely belongs to Mam, but she, lying there bloody and sweating after a too-quick two-hour delivery, a geriatric mother of 38 with her figure forever shot to hell and two young boys downstairs waiting for her to survive, well she isn't really in any condition to care about the fate of my afterbirth.

Shropshire was home to my grandparents too who had retired there after the smog of Leeds began to attack Granddad's chest. They made a harmonious pair: the tiny, sharp-eyed French-Canadian Yvette, who my mother was named for, and large, one-toothed Leeds-born Horace, who hated his name and was known by everyone as Jim. But within two years of my birthday my Mam had returned to Leeds. I secretly know why: Grandma left Mam alone for much of her pregnancy, finally coming around to her only slowly, and well after the messy birth was out of the way.

Whatever the reasons, she got over them, as I am sure Grandma loved me. But she loved me with the kind of clear-eyed severity with which she attacked her rows of potatoes when it was time to lift them and the compost heap when it needed turning. She was unbending and precise in her opinions, the kind of precision by which she reduced a marrow the size of a man's leg to tiny pieces one sixth of the size of a postage stamp when it was autumn and time to make marrow and ginger jam. Unbending in her view that the starving Biafrans on the telly 'didn't miss their children like us.... they just have another one'.

Certainly, there were many reasons for her to object to Mam's pregnancy: race, illegitimacy, single moth-erhood—Gran was a devout Catholic after all. And it appears she didn't want to know any more details which could compromise her further in the eyes of God than she was forced to. "Was the father black?" she asked Mam, for I was weeks old by then and the colour which couldn't be seen in my skin at birth had started to develop. I was gradually growing darker-skinned by the day. Mam confirmed that my daddy had indeed been black and that was the only conversation they ever had about him.

The 'we' who returned to Leeds to escape Gran's chilly hospitality comprised my pale, fine-haired Mam and two gangly boys of eleven and thirteen, her sons by her first marriage, who were extremely proud of their baby half-sister, the brown-eyed, brown-skinned fat-legged toddler that was me. This was the hodgepodge of a family that came back to Leeds, ready to make a home at Number 24. And this is the house I stand before now, a stranger looking up at the sightless windows and wondering what I expected to find here.

4.

Number 24

Back when I was at primary school, no one seemed to notice I'd come apart from myself. If my newly-detached personality had made her presence felt, then she simply wasn't mentioned. We were good at that, getting on with things, and after my shocking discovery, life at home carried on pretty much as usual at Number 24. This business-as-usual wasn't for want of my trying though, for I wasn't a self-effacing child.

In the early eighties our suburban castle is home to me, my Mam, my brother Paul and now only occasionally my brother Andrew. Andrew is thirteen years older than me and still the man of the house, even though he isn't actually here that much. Tonight, he is home on leave from the Army in which he will soon become a paratrooper. It won't be long before he will find himself landing at Port Stanley in the Falkland Islands on the deck of a battle-ready *QE2*. But on this evening, he is still a chef in the service and he has come to see us and left his chef's knives, of which he is inordinately proud, in a burgundy leatherette attaché case in the hall. Paul is nine years older than me. He is working at a clerical job for a local coach company, Wallace Arnold, and is rather in Andrew's shadow, where he will remain for the rest of his life.

We are in Number 24's ornate front room with its high, moulded ceilings, extra-wide door and other delusions of grandeur. A plump, nappy-haired golden-brown girl, I am too old to be lying on the orange furry rug, too close to our mahogany-cased television. I am blocking the heat from a belching and popping gas fire and wearing the remains of my school uniform with my pink, fluffy, mule slippers. I'm having my favourite after-dinner snack: chocolate digestives slid under the fire's grill and heated upon the narrow shelf in front of the flames until the chocolate bubbles. The fire is naughtily turned up full, even though it's June, but long June days in Yorkshire are rarely accompanied by warm nights and there is no central heating in this big, draughty monument of a house.

To a small girl, Number 24 appears vast and impressive. A Victorian semi rising over four floors, its nineteenth century façade looming over the mostly 1930s suburb of Kirkstall. The house is rich with detail: from the white, intricately-carved wooden porch to the deep fruit-and-flowers plaster coving in the front room. As well as reception rooms to the front and back, there are three bedrooms on the first floor, and another two built into the attic. At some point the sparsely-planted front garden was dug out and the cellar insulated and carpeted to make another bedroom, one which flooded frequently in wet weather. Altogether, six bedrooms are carved out of the carcass of Number 24 and the back reception, used as my Mam's bedroom, makes seven. As well as all these bedrooms, the house boasts an eat-in kitchen overlooking the long thin back garden. With its added-on dormers and mock-grandeur adornments, the house seems to look down on the neighbours like a prim Victorian matron strayed into the wrong neighbourhood. In such a big lumbering place, a small girl has to make a lot of noise to be heard at all. But now the noises I heard my mother making need to be talked about, even though it's something I know I can't mention. This presents a thoughtful girl with a puzzle.

Even if our house has a bit of an attitude, our street is respectable and respectability is important on our street, because only a couple of roads away lies a council estate of pot-bellied bungalows, shit-strewn pavements and front yards filled with cars and motorcycles reduced to their parts. Sited on a hill and so always on view, there is a constant tension between our private houses of owner-occupiers and this council estate, known locally as 'The Raynvilles'. As in, 'Well, you know, she lives in the Raynvilles' accompanied by an old-fashioned look and a meaningful pause.

We don't actually have Number 24 to ourselves. Our family occupies only the basement, ground floor and two of the first floor bedrooms. The biggest first floor bedroom and the two attic rooms house a carnival of lodgers, or 'the tenants' as we call them behind their backs. For Mam the tenants are essential to help pay the mortgage. For us they are an endless source of fascination. On the upper floors of Number 24 other worlds were regularly made and remade. I remember gently pushing back the door of one first floor bedroom and watching Tunde, a student from Cameroon silently, reverently, polishing his new shoes. One of our most glamorous tenants is Tunde—an absolute slave to fashion.

These shoes are showy platforms, emerald green with their seams contrast-stitched in white. He sits on the narrow single bed and there is little else in the room that was not already there when he paid Mam his first week's rent. Along with the bed, there are some rickety post-war utility drawers, a matching wardrobe and a sink in the corner with a Baby Belling hot plate standing on the laminate table beside it. Paul has become a good friend of Tunde's and he is very, very envious of these shoes.

Tunde moves his index finger round and round in tiny circles. He will spend ages buffing Cherry Blossom polish (shade: neutral) into them until they shine. Paul's envy justifies his purchase—even if the shoes were ridiculously expensive. Upon wearing them he will look down and see his square, blue-black face reflected back at him even more glamorously than before.

In a while Tunde will pick his way down the swirly hall carpet making enough noise on his stacked shoes that we, the family, will ease ourselves up out of sofas or struggle up from the fire-side rug to go into the hall and say goodbye. Of course we'll really be there to gawp. Nodding and asking after our health, Tunde will politely acknowledge our worship both arrogantly and humbly, as if waving at us enthusiastically but from a proper distance. Then with his brown leather jacket slung over one powerful shoulder and draping over his too-tight flared slacks, we'll get a final look at those shoes before he wishes us a polite good evening, and steps out into the Yorkshire night. We will sit on the tweed sofas and talk about him, because for us Tunde is the ultimate embodiment of cool.

5.
Monty

It is seven o'clock, and the weather has turned to freezing when I finally make it to see Mam. My legs shake a little as I walk toward her small block of flats. The ghosts of our little family are nipping at my heels, trying to join our party. I think my feet ache from pressing the accelerator to the floor for hours in my ancient car, but it could be the memories making their presence felt, pinching the muscles between my shoulders, making me notice how my fisted hands still grip an imaginary steering wheel. I try and stretch a little before pressing the intercom. The visit to Number 24 has made me more nervous, not less. The burdens of the past become more onerous.

There's no time to get my bearings. Steady myself. Before I can draw a breath Mam starts shouting from the speaker. "Hello? Hello?" she crackles, before pressing the buzzer to release the main door. I go in and glimpse Mam standing, back lit, in the doorway to her flat. She is tiny now, a little over four and a half foot. Her shrinking height is emphasised by the beginnings of curvature in her neck and shoulders. She begins to walk slowly toward me down the gloomy hallway, peering at the ground directly in front of her feet, searching for potential hazards.

We don't hug or touch, but when she tries to take my bag out of my hand with a withered fist, I tug it back. Then she says loudly: "Don't let Monty out!" before opening the interior door to her flat a ten-inch crack. We both squeeze through and I follow her into her immaculate living room while listening to her report on her health. Mam, walking so slowly, has plenty of time to describe her symptoms: a bad night because her back ached, her gums were sore and her waterworks have been playing up, forcing her to the bathroom several times.

When we finally make it through to the living room, the first thing I see is Monty asleep on the daybed. He is a giant marmalade tortoiseshell tom cat who is snoring gently into his special blanket. His stomach is so fat, his limbs thrust out in front and behind his impressive paunch, look too small. I wonder whether to risk waking him up with a scratch behind the ears—he is not the best tempered of creatures—and Mam notices me noticing him.

"I'm sure his head's getting smaller," she says,

"It's relative Mam. His head's looking smaller because his body is getting bigger."

Mam turns away. "Tea or coffee?" she says sharply, already holding the kettle under the tap. Her one-bedroom flat is tiny but pristine: it is little more than half-a-dozen arthritic steps from the Habitat daybed which holds Monty, to the two-seater Argos sofa occupied by Treacle, an undersized brown Tabby who is a mere three years old to Monty's fourteen. She opens one gimlet eye before leaping up and disappearing under the daybed, the better to observe me, the interloper. Now at least I can sit down, though it will be on a thin layer of Treacle's hair.

"I've been thinking of putting him on a diet, but the vet says he's healthy," Mam concedes.

"Well that's the important thing..." and I know to leave the subject alone.

Once we are settled with hot drinks—tea with milk for me, instant coffee with Coffee Mate and Sweetex for her—it's down to business. We are together to discuss her move into a new flat, three streets away.

"The survey has shown up there may be a problem with the roof ...," I start to explain.

"Do you want something to eat?" Mam suddenly asks. I know that any talk of solicitors, surveyors and estate agents is boring to her. She is already leaning back in her seat, the better to swing her weight forward to help in raising herself to her feet.

"No, I'm fine." I am determined not to be distracted.

"But you must be hungry?" Mam persists.

"No, I ate before I left."

"Have a cheese straw. They're Marks & Spencer's. I can put them in the oven to freshen them up a bit."

"No Mam, it's fine."

"Are you on a diet?"

"Err, well, I'm trying to watch my weight." Suddenly I know I've lost this round.

"Oh Kate, why are you dieting? You're gorgeous, everyone says so. Just have one, they're delicious. Look!"—by now she has the box out and is wafting the buttery-cheesy-pastry smells under my nose—"They're as light as a feather. And I have some crumbly Cheshire from the market".

In a moment she is bending painfully down in front of the fridge squinting at the contents because she isn't wearing her glasses and thrusting her right hand with its swollen knuckles into the bottom shelf, trying to grab the Cheshire cheese. Mam can move deceptively quickly when she wants to, and she usually wants to when food is involved.

"Why don't you do a plate for us to share?" I concede defeat quicker than usual, partly because I think she must be hungry and needs me to eat with her, and partly because I want to get the chat about the practicalities of buying the flat out of the way so we can talk about curtains, bedside lamps and carpets, all of which Mam has already chosen.

Mam is particularly excited because today is special. An auspicious start to the New Year is already in progress, because the Massey family, or what remains of it, will be together for the first time in almost two years. I can tell Mam is on edge. Her surviving children together in one room hardly ever happens.

Before the cheese pastries are out of the oven, the intercom goes again and I hear my brother's deep voice over the speaker. Andrew is fifty, an ex-paratrooper with a pink, weather-beaten face and the body of a man twenty years younger. He goes through the palaver of squeezing through the door with good grace and immediately seats himself on the sofa nearest the TV, where Mam usually sits. He shares her blue eyes and pronounced Roman nose and is now almost as fair as she. His father was Ricky, Mam's first husband, who died before I was born. Our brother's absence haunts the room. The remaining seat should be his, should be supporting his wraith-like body, his bright green eyes, his nervous smile.

We start talking over one another, the better to drown out his absence. We ask each other which route we took to the house, compare journey times, discuss each other's health, while Mam almost skips around the flat, making us fresh cups of tea and coffee, offering us chocolates and Turkish Delight on top of the cheese and biscuits, loving us in the best way she knows how.

She is as tiny and excited as a girl despite her arthritic hip, and her watery eyes sparkle. At five foot one I tower over her when I stand to take my tea.

After the bustle of arrivals, a silence falls. We are together so seldom that there are no natural grooves for the rhythm of our conversation. The subjects that can be talked about—my brother's children, his work, and less so, my work—have to be identified on the conversational hoof, there are no established rules. But we are managing, though it is hard work asking relevant questions and giving truthful—or more truthfully, near-truthful—answers, while the subjects we can't talk about, too numerous to mention, are nimbly avoided.

"So you've been to Marks & Spencer..." I say to Mam, spotting some new-looking M&S bags in the corner.

"I went this morning. There was nothing in the sale." Mam closes my conversation-starter down.

"Their men's stuff is so old-fashioned. I'm getting more into clothes now. I got this jumper from Next..." Andrew does his best.

"I got three tops. None of them in the sale though," Mam sniffs.

We go on like this for a while, pretending that we have no shared past and busy trying to establish a future we can deal with, even if only for one wintry evening. I am becoming anxious, anticipating that our chat about Marks & Spencer and the meal Mam has cooked—which we all agree is fabulous—will soon be exhausted. The anxiety, vague at first, soon begins an internal monologue. Perhaps all that can't be said will burst out of me? What if the subtexts to our small talk become so urgent, with neglect, with self-importance, that they leak from the margins to the centre of the conversation of their own accord? I am two people: one sat smilingly chatting, while the other listens to this stream of thought float through her consciousness. Then I relax for a moment and thoughtlessly rake a hand through my thick, curly hair and scratch my scalp.

My mother is quick: "Kate! Don't sit there scratching your head like a monkey."

Mam sometimes uses English in an unusual way, like a foreigner doing an (almost pitch-perfect) impression of a Yorkshire grandmother, which is exactly what she is. She doesn't mean this admonishment as it sounds, nevertheless I am about to tell her to mind her own business when my brother slides the milky-blue marbles of his eyes first to mine, then to Mam's. The timing between us is innate. I recognise the floor is his and close my mouth.

"Unfortunate choice of phrase" he says in advance of a smile that dramatically lights up his face. And we all laugh like drains, far more than the joke actually deserves. But it isn't a bad joke and it re-establishes us as intimates. An outsider saying such a thing to the white brother and mother of a mixed-race daughter would be unacceptably rude. Well, I think it would. And I assume Mam and Andrew agree. Though, troublingly, I can't be absolutely sure.

The next four hours' rush by: we talk over one another, under one another: I remember that my mother's company can be a particular pleasure when diluted by my brother. We all laugh a lot and the sadness I was anxious about, the sadness that flows not so far from the surface on our rare meetings, is subsumed in a tide of words. Andrew is not really one to visit much and he is not much of a talker on the phone, so there is a lot to fit in.

After we eat, Andrew takes his leave, and I comfort Mam, who is trying to stem tears which are ever-ready to fall in the presence of her surviving children. After another hour, I leave too, and she almost seems fine, but I know she will be sat on the sofa for a bit longer spilling more hot, salty tears for me. Then there will be some for our absent brother and the lost expression in his eyes.

As I drive back through the dark, I am shocked by the knowledge, the unassailable fact, that the tiny one-bedroom flat I have just left is a place where I am really loved. No matter that I am pushing forty and have long felt like Mam's parent. No matter how complex and mired in the events of the past that love might be.

6.

Choices

After Tunde leaves, Andrew and Paul are sat opposite me on the fluffy brown tweed-patterned settee. Neither is particularly tall but Andrew is much broader. He has fine dark hair, a prominent nose and chin, and a wide jaw that allows an exceptional smile to break through his ruddy face and crinkle the sides of his bright blue eyes. He's just told a joke and all three of us are laughing, but he most of all. Paul, sat next to him, shares our brother's features but on a smaller scale. The colouring's different too: Paul's hair is dark-blonde and his eyes are more green than blue. He is half Andrew's size and looks as if he may easily be picked up by a passing wind and carried away. He laughs too, but distractedly, and continues to stare attentively at the TV. He makes little eye contact with his brother or me, his unlikely-looking sister lying on the rug. The laughter is followed by a silence of anticipation.

"I could be so good for you. Love you like you want me to."

All three of us sing in time with the theme tune.

"There ain't nothing I can't go throughooooo…I'll be so good for YOU!"

We go on singing the theme tune until Arthur's griz-zled features and Terry's baby-smooth chops fill the 18-inch screen, then we are pretty much silent for the next fifteen minutes. It is not that the telly is so inter-esting it demands our full attention. It is more that all three of us sat down and watching the telly together is too precious to talk through.

Then Andrew says: "Make us a cup of tea Paul", and it's barely a question, more an expectation. Paul hauls himself up scowling and makes his way into the kitchen. Andrew and I know he will struggle to make tea in the two-and-a-half minutes the adverts take before the start of Part Two.

With my hair made static by the orange rug and sticking out of my head in all directions, I follow Paul to the scullery kitchen at the back of the house, awkwardly carrying three dirty tea mugs. This kitchen will eventu-ally undergo a modernisation to enlarge the small window overlooking the back garden and replace the hodge-podge of brown laminate cupboards with clean-looking shiny ones. But for now it is dark, tunnel-like.

At the end of the gloom, framed in the window with her back to me, stands the five-foot figure of my Mam. The remains of the mid-summer sunlight streams through her bouffant red-brown hair. Her shoulders are hunched over the stainless steel sink as she half-heartedly extracts clean pots from it one by one and places them on the drainer. She's looking out onto the garden. During these light nights, her blue eyes, identical to Andrew's, fix on the stretch of lawn running up to the garage at the end of the garden. The lawn is edged by raspberry bushes that by the end of the summer holidays will be bent into hoops with the weight of turgid fruit.

She looks down into my brown eyes, fatigue etched into her fleshy pale face. "Are you going to bed soon, my little butterball?"

She bends to take the tea mugs off me.

"Nooooooo. Maaam. After *Minder*."

Our talk is as usual, but I am changed, and I look deeper into her pale eyes, willing her to notice that despite the boys sitting on the sofa, the telly being on, the tea we've just had and the cuppa Paul's making, despite everything being as usual, I will never be the same again. I am ready for a dramatic confrontation—in fact, I've planned it. Mam will give me the cue by saying something like: "I can tell there's something wrong, what is it Kate?" like people do in soap operas. She will say this in close-up with a concerned expression. Then I will tell her what I heard when Sarah and I were stood on the front step, and I will ask her what it means, and find out if it has anything to do with our phone ringing much more than it used to, and the doorbell going a lot and the strange men stood on the doorstep I have seen from my bedroom window. The tenants have visitors, yes, but never so many as this. Suddenly our house, and I suspect, our Mam, is much more popular than before.

I keep on staring at her, silently imploring her to see that I am now only of a fraction of what I was. "When you go back in the room, tell Andrew the lawn needs cutting," she says, turning back to the sink and her thoughts have already moved on.

She's tired, but not as tired as when she worked in an office and came home and shouted at me. If I asked her a question—and maybe, I asked a lot of questions—she'd shout: "I'm tired Kate!" As if I didn't know. If not fatigue, then why doesn't she notice? Perhaps it's because I look too different for her to read my expression. Besides her frank gaze and habit of raising her eyebrows in emphasis, I see nothing of my own shiny yellow-brown face and frizzy hair in Mam's pasty colouring. Andrew has Mam's nose with its distinct bulge at the tip. And Paul, who's stood next to the gas hob glaring at the kettle because it won't boil quickly enough, well, he has more of her temperament than she is willing to admit. She dries the last of the pots from dinner, nudges Paul away from the cooker and takes over making the tea.

In a bit, she'll sit down with us in the front room in her armchair under the standard lamp with the cream tart's bloomers shade. She'll sew, taking up a hem with tiny stitches, or she'll read the small ads in *The Yorkshire Evening Post*.

Looking after us and No 24 is hard work and we don't begrudge her a sit down. After the meals have been cooked, the tall house cleaned from top to bottom and beds made. After two sudden marriages and a just-as-sudden divorce, at this moment Mam is alone and I am glad.

I am glad that Tom has gone. Tom, who I had to call Daddy, but who was not my daddy or anything close to it. Tom has gone and will not be coming back. Roy has gone as well. It was struggle for Mam to get rid of that one, but he is finally history. I am not sorry to see the back of either of them, and these nights when Andrew brings his easy laugh back from Camp and Mam sits down with us to watch telly are chances to pretend that I am still the baby of the family.

Soon it'll be time for me to haul myself up off the rug and go upstairs to my narrow room. The boys will follow not long after and Mam last of all, turning off lights and locking the back door. One last look out into the dark of the garden where the long grass mocks her housekeeping, then off to a lonely but longed-for rest for her too.

I lie in bed and think, for I have a lot of thinking to do, and bed is the best place for it. I lie for a long time, contemplating ghostly wallpaper roses in the dark, not reading or listening to Radio Luxembourg, just lying. It is true that now I get more of Mam's time. She doesn't believe in playing with children but she sometimes watches old films with me. Tomorrow's the Saturday Matinee on BBC2. Jeanette MacDonald and Nelson Eddy, Micky Rooney, Doris Day or Bette Davis. A musical would be a treat: *Calamity Jane*, or *South Pacific*,

Mam's favourite, or *The King & I*, mine. But now I can't relax and the film won't be so much fun.

I didn't know I had been enjoying growing up. No idea that reading *Jackie*, *My Guy* and *Blue Jeans*, giggling over boys and learning the lyrics to my favourite pop songs had been so much fun. The days before I found out about Mam's new business seem a childhood away and it is time for me to put away childish things. I have a new task. I must manage Mam and her secret. Someone's got to get us through this, Andrew is in the army and Paul's just not up to it. So it will have to be me.

7.
Playing Out

Playing out was how I discovered the world beyond 24 Victoria Park Avenue. It was a world away from how Andrew and Paul played with me. Their idea of play was teasing me mercifully, nicknaming me Granny Gunge, because I was serious and opinionated. Sometimes, they let me join in with them. I could occasionally sit quiet in the kitchen when Paul's few friends came to the house in their black t-shirts and leather jackets and talked excitedly about Hondas, horsepowers and CCs. Occasionally, I would help Andrew with something practical: collecting manure for the raspberry bushes from the nearby stables for instance. While we shovelled straw-filled shit into black bin bags, Andrew would call 'Dung, dung! Round one!' intermittently just to make me laugh. In this way, Andrew and Paul occasionally allowed the door to their world to fall open a crack, before they remembered I was a child, and a girl, and slammed it shut again. Before I was old enough to play out by myself, about 8 years old, Andrew, then in his early 20s, left home to join the army. Paul would be around for a little while yet, but was for the moment absorbed by his passion for motorbikes.

Playing out was my world, separate from my family. It was a world that became bigger as I pushed the boundaries of my playground, beyond our cul-de-sac and into the wider streets of Leeds. A grubby child may have knocked at the front door and been answered by my harried Mam. She'll hear the kid ask "Is Katy playing out?" but before the question mark is out between her ice-pop stained lips, Mam will already be calling me downstairs. Mam doesn't like me to have my head buried in a book and so will shortly be shoving me out to play with this doorstep Huckleberry. Times are different now. Today, such behaviour is worse than ridiculous—it is dangerous, not only from the risk of injury, of which I had quite a few, or 'stranger-danger', but the notion that your child could go out into the world and independently choose their playmates is a threat that potentially allows God-knows-who into the heart of the home. But back then that was how we made friends; playing out was both the means and solution to our social lives.

It started with the street in front of our house: I was allowed to go as far as Binns' newsagents down the hill, and the end of Victoria Park Avenue up the hill. In between was my playing out kingdom of about a dozen ragtag and bobtail kids who knocked a ball about using jumpers to mark the goal posts, we would form a chain across the street for violent but fun games of British bulldog, or spend our days bickering about who took turns holding the rope for Double Dutch skipping.

But even before Mam's secret set me apart, I was often alone. The games that I played alone were important to me: I made the rules, and only I judged the risks. This was when I was at my most grown-up, my most in control. One day when I was about nine years old, a day that is still physically imprinted on my forehead, I spent an afternoon repeatedly jumping off the wall in front of Number 24. I climbed up onto the wall—not high, about three and a half foot—and tottered there for a moment, catching my balance, before jumping down onto the pavement with a satisfying thud. This kept me interested for a while, but once the jump was mastered I had to make it more interesting. I puzzled, then inspiration struck—I would jump off the wall backwards! I was confident, but newly serious in the face of what I perceived, rightly as it turned out, to be a serious challenge to my athleticism.

I clambered onto the wall again. This time, I turned to face the bay window before steadying myself in a crouched position. Head down, I took a breath, held it, closed my eyes and jumped up, up into thin air; for a second I was suspended in time. I landed safely on the pavement. But I hadn't propelled myself backwards enough. I bent my knees to absorb the landing and at the same time leaned forward and head-butted the coping stone on the top of the wall.

I lie stunned for a second, then pain flooded in. I put my hands up to my forehead and made my way through the house wailing. I had to find Mam: only she could persuade my bloody hands away from the injury. She took a good look at the small, triangular wound and pronounced that it wasn't life threatening. I couldn't believe it. My head was agony. My tear-streaked, screwed-up snotty face must have begged a more serious diagnosis, because then Mam said, hastily, that the wound *was* serious enough to warrant a plaster. I wore the pale pink plaster across the middle of my brown forehead for days. And, for once, Andrew and Paul didn't take the piss.

I was soon to break the boundary of Binns' newsagents, finding newer and more dangerous playgrounds. I played at a railway siding, moving what I obscurely thought of as 'gears' but now know to be point switchers, and using my arms to balance my pudgy body as I twirled along a track, pretending to be Nadia Comenci on the beam. I would play by the Leeds-Liverpool canal which runs along the bottom of Victoria Park Avenue, passed the nearby brewery which salted the air with the pleasant warm stench of yeast and hops. At the canal I found that, from between the Morrisons' trolleys, old prams and dead dogs, it was possible to catch tiddlers in a net. I would bring them home in a bucket for Mam. She admired my efforts, then flushed them down the toilet.

One of my final playgrounds, from near the end of my playing out days, was Kirkstall Abbey. The Abbey was an impressive ruin, of which enough remained to feed my imagination about the lives of the monks who lived there. But it was less the Abbey itself than the land surrounding it which fascinated me. It stood in acres of parkland, bounded on one side by the main road leading to the retail park, and on the other by the canal. There was also a river with a weir and an interesting collection of ramshackle buildings. One was a boarding kennel where restrained dogs barked energetically when I passed. There were also some sheds for a light railway on which a tiny engine pulled a couple of miniature carriages the mile or so from the Abbey to the back of British Home Stores, then back again.

The railway was good, but what I really liked to do was explore the boundaries of the Abbey grounds. I walked beside the river until the paths became so overgrown I frightened myself, because I could no longer see the ground beneath my feet. I clambered up parts of the ruin which were reduced to rocky outcrops so that I could see further into the distance, across the Abbey grounds to the rugby pitches and Bramley Fall Woods.

I still dream often of this piece of wild hinterland between the medieval lay-brother's quarters and the waterways of the industrial revolution. In my dream-memory, I cross the river on stepping stones and on the other side find an old churchyard, beautiful and decaying, where I wonder alone, crushing hillocky grass noiselessly beneath my feet. Here I linger, reading weathered inscriptions, peering into the lives of those long-dead.

I have tried to walk this path since and find it no longer exists, or it is not the way I remembered it, or it was never there at all. Trying to walk the landscape of dreams means that one or the other—the landscape or the dream itself—will be lost. It is impossible to revisit and retain both. But I hung onto my playing out world longer than I should have. The whole point of playing out was its purposelessness; I played because I played. Sometimes I won and sometimes I lost whatever game we started, whatever bet I had with myself. But the important thing was that tomorrow the playing out would continue right up until the sunset if I wanted.

Then, quickly, stealthily, a different kind of competition emerged, one that was played out between girls for the boys' attention, a game where winning became far more loaded than who would be 'it' or who should turn the rope. Playing out gradually changed into hanging around Morrisons shopping centre and flirting with boys from Gotts Park High School. I wasn't ready for the shift, and still craved the rules I understood, unlike the nudging and giggling which suddenly seemed more important than cats' cradles. I guess my friends from the street were still playing when they flirted and smoked by the tennis courts, and would perhaps eventually play themselves into each other's arms. But, for me, to play implies the ability to escape oneself, to escape one's circumstance and I fear I stopped being able to escape the day my childish self floated away.

8.

Fat

Fat was something to be feared in our family and I carry that fear still. I worry when I put on weight I won't be able lose it, and I worry when I lose it that I will put it back on. My fatness was a matter of family lore, my weight a frequent conversation topic between my mother and my two brothers. Mam and Andrew even argued about it—as if my size was somehow her fault. If we discussed it now I would tell him that it was much more complex than Mam simply feeding me too much. My eating was structurally produced by the dynamics of my family. It was simply an output of the way things worked. There were dominant forces and vested interests taking sides in the question of whether I ate salad or chips.

Professionals became involved early on. My first visit to a nutritionist took place when I was eight years old and weighed eight and a half stones.

"What is this Katy?" that nice nutritionist lady asked me.

"A carrot," I said.

"This is *Percy* Carrot," she corrected, bravely rejecting

a more alliterative name. I noticed that Percy Carrot did indeed have a face and little legs. "Do you like to eat Percy Carrot?"

"Yes"

She asked me my opinion about a number of other foods, then I was instructed to colour in Percy Carrot along with a lot of other anthropomorphized fruit and vegetables while she talked to my mother, assuming that the act of vaguely scribbling with an orange felt-tip would temporarily render me deaf.

"The problem is not that Katy likes the wrong type of food. It's that she likes all food," the nutritionist diagnosed to my mother, who nodded sagely, with the serious look she always wore in the presence of experts. She told my mother I needed to eat more Percy Carrots and less cake, sweets, chops, roast dinners and everything else that Mam liked to cook. And so cured, we went home. At home I was to sit through many versions of our trip as it was related endlessly to friends and acquaintances.

"Katy is fat because she likes food too much." The myth was repeated time and time again until it became true.

It wasn't as if I had no example of dieting to work from. Mam dieted all the time. She frequently blamed my late birth for ruining her figure. I have an image of her lying on the bed, one arm raised to her brow like a tragic heroine, crying: "I'm ten stone two and I'm starving."

The nutritionist's diet didn't work for any length of

time and nor have all the others I have tried over the last thirty years or so. The damage had already been done. I haven't always been fat. I didn't grow organically through bonny babyhood, to pudgy toddler, through fat child to podgy adult. I was deliberately made fat. I was to be the fat one, the one who ate without knowing when to stop, the one who might have grown pretty despite and perhaps because of the obvious flaw of blackness, and thus, lest I wasn't socially impoverished enough, I was to be made obese.

The chief suspect in this crime was my mother's second husband, the improbably named Tom Jones. This made my mother Mrs Jones for a while and I got my first Step Daddy, though not, thank God, his name. There existed a picture of the three on us on their wedding day. My mum is in a dress of coffee-and-crème lace to just below the knee. She is holding me in her arms, a normal-sized toddler in a red velvet dress reaching out to something she is holding away from me. Tom has his arm around my Mam. He has gingerish hair, gold-rimmed glasses and is smiling as he squints into the camera, trying to keep the sun out of his eyes.

Before the ink was dry on the register it became obvious Tom was a liar and a con-artist who had married my mother because she was at the time fairly well-off; a widow, with a widow's pension and several properties which were rented out to students. He found excuses, then told outright lies to explain his lack of a job and bad luck in never being able to get one.

Tom lied compulsively, almost without knowing it was happening. These lies often served no purpose, were not to protect himself and gave him no apparent gain. Such lies eat away at their victim. My mother's world, her marriage and relationship, became unknowable to her, and robbed her life of any measure of predictability. The marriage lasted less than two years, and in that time I was transformed from a normal toddler into a child who would wear the label of obesity for the rest of her life.

It was done like this. Tom would buy me endless sweets and titbits. This demonstrated to my mother that he cared about me. I would, to gain praise and to show I was returning this affection, eat them. Then Tom would tease me. He liked to tease me by tickling me until I cried. Or he would squeeze my head between his legs until I cried.

He would catch my head as I passed him, clamping his knees hard around my ears. "Do you submit?" he'd say. And I would scream and cry but refuse to submit until it hurt too much. Then, when I had cried enough, he would give me more sweets.

Crying and eating were synonymous in my experience of this man. Tom caused pain, then provided the means of soothing that pain, becoming both comforter and tormentor. Finally, when I cried to my Mam, probably because Tom had hurt me, she gave me something to eat to cheer me up.

Given the nature of my own fattening, it confuses me as to why extreme over-eating isn't treated as both a mental and physical condition. Perhaps it is because the extremely thin engender pity, whereas the extremely fat incite contempt. Guilty contempt perhaps, but loathing nevertheless.

I am as bad as anyone. I saw an acquaintance in the street recently. It was a sunny day and people were reacting with exaggerated gratitude for the fine weather. Café tables had been put out into the street. Men and women sat on benches for no other reason than to bask. Then suddenly, almost beside me, was a woman I'd shared a house with for a while. There had been six of us in the house and I hadn't got to know her particularly well and the bits I did know of her I didn't particularly like. I cannot be sure that some of that antipathy had nothing to do with most of her bits being of larger-than-average size.

She wasn't huge then—a size eighteen to twenty perhaps. Now though, she had swelled. She half-shuffled, half-glided along the pavement. The fat which undulated softly, almost magisterially around her middle masked the huge effort it must have cost her to keep the dense mass of flesh vertical and in forward motion.

One swollen foot uncomfortably followed another as she passed, appearing not to see me, as I appeared not to see her. The lie of this was underscored by her new size. She had crossed a threshold that all fat people (or used-to-be-fat people, or afraid of being fat people) will recognise.

The threshold is one where a person stops being buxom, well-covered or simply overweight, and passes into the territory of huge, gargantuan, grotesque. This is the space one occupies when one's size embarrasses people. This woman had become so big that though everyone in the street that warm day could hardly have failed to see her, she was rendered strangely invisible. The observers' fear simply erased her. My reaction was first shock, then paralysis, as acknowledging her became impossible.

Perhaps that's why, in all my battles with my body, I have always been able to buy clothes in 'normal' shops. I have never crept above a size eighteen without being successful enough at one diet or another to reduce my body to more acceptable proportions. On one liquid diet, I lost a stone and a half in six weeks. I resumed eating solids when my blood pressure dropped and my body hair stopped growing. Even so, the memory of the power I gained over my appetite then is still a sweet one.

9.

The Day She Nearly Left

One day Mam came in from work with a dark expression on her face. I had been home from school a little while and lay, as usual, on the hearth rug eating biscuits in front of *Blue Peter*. Mam looked as if she was going to come into the room, but she stopped at the doorway, and just stood there, as if something was stopping her coming any closer. She looked weird, like a black cloud in a dress. She was looking at me but didn't really see me. I expected her to turn the fire down to miser rate, the lowest setting, but she didn't. She just stood there.

I already knew Mam wasn't happy. I knew this because every day before going to school and every day before going to bed I found her on her knees repainting the Anaglypta wallpaper that covered the hall wall on all three floors of our house. She used a two-inch brush and never had a mark of the white gloss paint on her blue overall. She painted and painted, but she wasn't really a person for DIY—that was my oldest brother Andrew's job anyway—so this was odd. We three pretty much looked after ourselves while she was: 'Getting on with the painting'.

But sometimes I found her on the first floor outside the bathroom, or sometimes she'd be high in the eaves of the attic. This seemed a strange way to tackle the job. That is, if you must put more white on a wall which was already white, which only a grown up would think of doing. Anyway, while she was painting the Anaglypta and half-heartedly forcing the oozing paint into the bubbled-up pattern she had the same look as she is wearing now.

"Kate get up and get your coat. We're going out."

"Maaam..." I whined. Usually she hated this, but this time she didn't really hear me. It was early for grown-up going out and late for me to go out. In any case, children's programmes were still on. *Captain Pugwash* hadn't even started yet. I wouldn't have minded if she'd waited until the *News*. Also, I'd been cold on the way home from school and it was warm and comfy in front of the fire.

"We're. Going. Out!"

She turned and walked slowly, weirdly, out of the room. I knew something was really wrong: she hadn't even noticed the fire. I hauled myself up from the rug and turned it off. I knew better than to argue so I put my duffle coat on and waited by the door. After a minute, Mam drifted down the hall toward me wearing the pale-blue, double-breasted raincoat that was big enough for her to wrap me inside when it was cold at the bus stop. She said nothing as she took my hand. We walked out the front door into flinty winter air.

"Where're we going Mam?"

"To the pictures."

And she was as good as her word. We went to see *Digby: The Biggest Dog in the World* which I had already seen the week before. I didn't tell her this because Mam and I never go to the pictures together. Mam or Andrew sometimes took me to the Lounge Cinema at 9.30 on Saturday mornings. Quite often one of them is there to pick me up at noon. The pictures is something I do on my own, but there are loads of other kids there. We watch cartoons, black and white Children's Film Foundation serials, though we all have colour tellies, and there is a main film and last week it was *Digby*. Also, we eat sweets and some kids throw them or popcorn at each another, which is a waste.

But this wasn't like that. Mam said this was a treat and I got a tub of ice cream from the lady who carried a box of them in front of her and there were lots of grownups there with their children and the pictures was quiet and organised. I really liked *Digby*. It's about a sheepdog who gets so big a boy about my age has to actually get inside his mouth and pour antidote down his throat to make him normal size again. I also like Jim Dale who is in *Digby*, and also in the *Carry On* films. I didn't mind seeing it again.

I was enjoying it second time as well, which is unusual, but then I turned around to look at Mam to see if she was laughing. She wasn't, and her face was pointing at the screen but she wasn't watching it, I could tell.

After the pictures I thought we would go home. Paul would be back and I still had my uniform on, which was itchy. But when walked out into the street Mam said: "Do you want to go to the Wimpy for egg and chips?" even though it was dark and most of the cars had gone.

I had already had biscuits and milk and the ice-cream and was a bit tired, but somehow I knew she wanted me to say yes so that's what I did. At the Wimpy I got egg and chips and a milkshake and tried to eat all of it because Mam was watching me over her cup of tea and I wanted to make her happy by enjoying the food. And she did smile. But it wasn't a happy one and there were still clouds in her eyes even though it was night.

The nice waitress who'd brought my food and Mam's tea started cleaning tables near us. Everyone else had gone. She smiled at my Mam but Mam looked down. The waitress smiled at me, and I looked at her properly and grinned back so she'd know we were OK, and not mad or anything, and would be going soon. She came and stood next to our table.

"Can I take these?" she said, pointing to the dirty crockery.

"Yes. Yes, we're just going," Mam said, but didn't try to put her coat on, even though we had nothing left to eat. I was feeling a bit sick because of all the food, and it was obvious the place was closing and I was starting to feel a bit embarrassed.

"You got any more?" asked the nice waitress, gesturing at me with a saucer.

"Two boys," Mam's voice was squeaky and breathy at the same time as if she'd squeezed it out on a sigh. I could see her eyes getting all watery and I thought she might cry. But before I could think about how to get us out before the tears came the lady said:

"You know love, I've had six. But I've never had a brown one." Then the waitress and Mam both started to laugh. I was so relieved I joined in too, even though I thought it was a silly thing to say and the nice waitress had gone down a little in my estimation.

After this we went home. After this, my step-daddy Tom left. And he was gone for good this time, Mam said. Then, after a while, her painting stopped as well, and it was safe again. Safe to run downstairs and trail my fingers against the cool folds of shiny white Anaglypta without worrying that the gloss would come off on my hands.

10.

I Hardly Knew You

I knew that my real Daddy hadn't quite completely left. Despite the arrival and departure of two step-fathers in quick succession, despite hardly ever seeing him, despite hearing his name only rarely (and then always uttered through a scowl), I knew he was still around. And, if not close, then at least he was never too far away. If Jamaica was not too far away. And if me and Mam didn't know where he was sometimes, then it was likely that he was closer than Jamaica, and crucially, well within saving-Katy distance: for I might need him at any moment. And then he would appear, sweeping his Khaki Princess into his arms, saving his best until last, like in books. And this was the most important thing: I learned that through sheer force of will, I could somehow keep him by. I just had to try and keep on trying, for if I relaxed for a minute, a second, I might forget him and then he would be gone.

Cyril Anglin, my father, was born, I think, in Kingston Jamaica, and I am told he manned US submarines during the Second World War. But why did he come to Britain? And for what? I still don't fully know. True he was not alone, and he came at a time when joining the wind-ward rush East was an opportunity for young single West Indian men. But it's not enough, doesn't cover it. He was not so young anyway. He was not single, as far as I know. My sparse memories of him are of a man who wouldn't have been seen dead driving a bus or checking a tube ticket. And he was not poor either, or so he said, because he had land in Jamaica and work in America. I have no idea what my Daddy was doing here, only that maybe his brothers came here too, and they all lived in London.

So I hardly knew him, but I have a small collection of memories which I keep safely wrapped in my subconscious to emerge in dreams or while I am poorly with a bad cold, or sometimes when friends talk about their fathers, now aged and grown bad-tempered or babyish. These memories—or rather bits of memories, for they are not even complete stories—embarrass me, like a childhood collection of bus tickets or sea glass re-discovered in the corner of a loft. These memories, like those out-of-date tickets and smooth shards, resemble nothing more than rubbish when stripped of the passion that brought them together in the first place. But I know what I recall is paltry compared to the love I have put into their careful storage away from the harsh light of day, and the effort of cleaning and polishing I have poured into keeping them fresh.

For instance: I remember the feel of his hair—a tight afro sparsely distributed over his smooth, dark mahogany skull. I can see my infant hand reaching out in front of my face to touch this hair. I had never experienced a texture like it: it was rough like sandpaper, much rougher than my hair, even though it was the same colour. But press a little harder and it was soft and springy as well, like Mam's sheepskin rug when I buried my hand properly in, past the candyfloss softness down to the tightly-packed hair nearest the skin. I also remember a pair of bell-bottomed trousers he bought me. I must have been about five years old. They were purple corduroy with triangular panels of purple floral fabric near the bottom, which meant the trousers flared out in a satisfying, swingy way. He also bought me a blouse that matched the floral panels. Sashaying down the street, I thought I looked like Latoya or Janet off *The Jacksons*. I felt ten foot tall in those trousers.

I have a couple of other memories: I once stayed with him and Auntie Hortense and my cousins in London. I remember Hortense—a large woman whose smile and voice were even bigger than her behind, a kind woman who gave me cordial made with sugar, water and food colouring which I hated and fried chicken which I loved. Daddy took me to The Planetarium while I was in London—I don't know why, I clearly recall that I really wanted to go to Madame Tussauds, but we ended up at the Planetarium anyway.

I was enraptured. I saw all the stars and planets, Orion's Belt and a full eclipse, but when I turned to look at my father, who I wanted to share my wonder, he had fallen asleep. He snored gently, his hat tipped down in front of his face. I resent that hat now, even though in my memory he is always, always wearing it. I hate that hat because it covered a face I can no longer bring to mind.

Because, though what I can actually recollect of him are sparse and scattered belongings, his continuing absence was part of the material of my life. For me, our household's father-shaped hole was a constant presence, like the regular beat of background music. I am pretty sure that it was true for my brothers as well, though, of course, their Daddy was not mine, my Daddy belonged to me and to me alone.

Andrew, Paul and me trod carefully around the place a man we felt *should have been*, busy making choices for us, protecting us. We made do with Mam as if she alone were a poor substitute for a perfect, whole family. Until an old photograph, a song, the smell of hair oil, until memory at any moment would trigger the presence of our terminally absent fathers, and the private music of our loss would drown out the noise of our everyday lives, dissolving us into tears or driving us to anger with its rhythmic urgency.

So, when my Daddy actually did die, it was like a second death to me, or perhaps it was rather that his death had never happened at all. A voice on the telephone which only days before (it seemed days to the eight-year-old me, but time was so malleable. A maths lesson lasted a day, whereas English ran for only ten minutes or so) told me that my father was very ill, now said: "You father is dead." It was a stranger's voice with a heavy Jamaican accent. Mam said it was my uncle, my father's brother, but to me it could have been anyone.

"I suppose I should go to his funeral," I said to Mam, through tears of incomprehension and a feeling no one articulated but that nevertheless weighed down on me. Was it duty? And why this feeling, toward a father who, through all that he had done, or rather had failed to do, had demonstrated absolutely that he hadn't known the meaning of the word?

Mam was typically succinct:

"It's a bit late to play the dutiful daughter now."

And that was the last we spoke of him for years.

My reaction was to turn my small shards of recollections into something else: a sense-memory, a feeling of him. He felt to me then like the scratchy part of the washing-up sponge, the smell of Black & White Pomade and the hard woolly fabric of fusty-smelling men's suits when I brushed against them in charity shops.

There are some things I chose to forget. Like how, on the few occasions that we talked face to face, he looked at me with eyes the detail of which I can no longer describe. As I answered his questions he would seem to only half-listen to what I said. While I talked, he rolled his eyeballs away and chewed slightly on the side of his mouth— a mouth which seemed perpetually to be in motion.

This is what I remember of him, an impression, I, then, consciously expunged. It is a kind of coarseness, his misunderstanding. He didn't understand any of it: me, the job my mother was doing bringing me up, what he should have done. Like he didn't know how to be a father. I don't know who rejected whom: my mother claims it was she who did so, but then Daddy certainly didn't fight for me and perhaps he was relieved when Mam said she wouldn't marry him.

These details hardly impinge though, because my instinct has never been to forget, seize the present, leave the dead to the past. Rather it is to keep safe my recollections and my fantasies, so that these sad baubles are maintained and polished, picked over and, in the repetition of the conscious act, regularly renewed. For I know it to be true: that what survives of us is love. The borderline of being and not being is policed by memory. A heartbeat, his pulse, is neither here nor there.

11.
Waterloo Bridge

Mam and I are laughing ourselves stupid at Vivien Leigh. Negligee-clad and perfectly made-up, she kneels, sobbing out her heart into an over-stuffed pouffe. Vivien is trying to explain to her future mother-in-law that she has been working as 1941's least likely prostitute. But good taste dictates opacity. This means Leigh can't just say that she was initially reluctant, but approaching punters asking: "Have you got a light soldier?" became preferable to starving. And anyway she believed her lover, played by Robert Taylor and thus unaccountably American, was missing in action.

"Moira, what's the matter? Is there another man?" implores the older woman, annunciating theatrically over her rectangular wall of a bosom.

"Oh Lady Margaret. You're so naïve," cries the unfortunate Vivien, further dampening the pouffe's damask. Now her true love has returned from the war unscathed, his passion for her undiminished, a world of respectability and privileged comfort is within her grasp. If only Vivien could have kept her mouth shut.

I am back in Leeds to watch *Waterloo Bridge* with Mam. We need to talk about her new flat of course, and I have a new plan to reveal to her: one which might suit both of us very well if we can make it work. But so we can talk *about* things, Mam and I have long communicated *through* other things. So I have driven down to have lunch with her and brought the DVD of our favourite tearjerker with me. I suggested watching the movie in our usual pre-visit telephone chats. These are critical negotiations where we discuss every aspect of our planned meeting.

So, the day before I'm due to go to Leeds, the phone rings for the fourth time. There's no need for 'hellos'. She's straight in.

"Do you want chops for lunch Kate? Or langoustines?... They're big prawns."

I do not know how to answer, I am in the middle of writing an article and my deadline is approaching like a line of infantry. But Mam needs to pin everything down. The next morning I am late setting off and rush around the flat throwing my purse into a bag, trying to find house-keys. The phone screams for attention again and I consider just walking away. But I don't.

"Will your allergy be OK with Monty here? I've bought some Piriton. Or should I wash the sofa covers, just in case?"

She is solicitous to a ridiculous degree, always 'just in case'. In case I am starving on arrival, so weakened by hunger I can't lift the telephone receiver to order Kung

Po chicken from the Chinese takeaway across the street. In case my occasional itchy-eye allergy to cats becomes anaphylaxis. In case we are faced with a moment not filled with the premeditated and the pre-arranged, a minute or two which demand improvisation. Such a moment could easily derail our conversation, send us hurtling into the conflict zones: the territory which lay at the periphery of our relationship. These darklands border the clear broad tracks of our everyday chat: a margin-country of lightless woodland and wordless humiliations.

I can't remember when we first saw *Waterloo Bridge*, or even if the first time I saw it was with Mam. The story is of a ballet dancer who runs away from the corps to marry an officer in the British army, but who sinks into prostitution after she believes he has been killed in action. We can quote the script almost word for word. *Waterloo Bridge* is but one missile in our armoury. There are other weapons, some relatively benign, some jagged and sharp, with which we arm ourselves for daily conversation.

For instance, we both regularly treat ourselves to an expensive ready-meal, usually from Marks & Spencer. Then we tell each other, via a detailed critique on its shortcomings, why we chucked it into the bin and made an omelette instead. We discuss over and over the difficulty of finding clothes to fit our plump, dumpy bodies. Her passion for clothes means Mam, even in her late-seventies, still drapes herself with the best and most flattering garments Leeds has to offer. But this is no shopping competition: it is a hunt. The thrill comes from spending the least amount of money.

We compete for bargains from charity shops, Primark and Dotty Perkins, the highest honours going to the one who has spent least on the most impressive item. When we meet we often bring the meat of our conversation with us. Mam, on her less and less frequent trips to see me, will bring a piece of a cake she's just baked, or half an excellent pork pie. These items will have nestled in her handbag against the remains of a packed lunch: a squashed and bruised banana perhaps or a pear weeping from its wounds. So on this visit I arrive with not only the DVD, but also a bag of past bargains destined for the RSPCA shop (because Mam likes to sort through them first to see if there's anything salvageable). Today, laden with my prizes, I am an exhausted lioness dragging a gazelle to its lair: the long throat ripped out, its horned head dragging leadenly against the ground.

But *Waterloo Bridge* has saved us again it seems. We can re-sheath our swords, at least for today. We have stopped laughing by the time Vivien stands on the bridge, traffic rattling past, her huge mad eyes staring into the fog-bound Thames. Mam and I know she won't tip herself in. No, she won't use the damp river. She will instead turn her back to the water and pause a moment before throwing herself in front of a military truck. The propaganda message is hardly subtle. "Housewives of Briton, look at the fate that awaits should you be tempted to supplement your coupons with a bit of lucrative how's-your-father."

As the credits roll, I shift in my seat, expecting Mam to begin her usual bustle, to ask me if I'd like a cup of tea, but she is still. I turn to look at her and she is staring at the TV, lost in her thoughts. Her features have softened. She is in a moment, her guard is down. Ever vigilant, the warrior within me senses an opportunity.

I start badly. "Are you sorry Mam? You know, about....." There is too much to say but at least I have almost, nearly, managed to ask the question. I hold my breath and admire my own courage. I should have instead thought about what I expected her to say. In combat, lack of preparation is the most obvious and avoidable mistake.

She snaps out of her reverie and turns and looks at me hard. In that instant I realise the scale of my miscalculation. Then eventually, briskly, almost as an afterthought she replies.

"Only that I'm not more sorry."

I am stunned at so much revelation in such a short, brutal sentence. She has thought about it. I am still dazed as she rushes on.

"Now," she pulls herself together with a single word, "do you want a cup of tea?"

12.
Fred Perry

I was a child who now had an important job to do. I had to stop my Mam's business seeping into my life. And yet machinations were going on in the background. I knew nothing of these plans until Mam asked one day: "How would you feel about going to boarding school, Katy?"

I was twelve and all I knew about boarding schools I had learnt from an early addiction to Enid Blyton's Mallory Towers books. From these I knew that boarding schools had fierce matrons in starched white uniforms, and there would be thrilling midnight feasts and I'd play posh games like hockey and lacrosse. It was the answer to my prayers. Boarding school would mean I could give up my exhausting day-to-day surveillance of Mam and start getting on with life. Since his marriage, Andrew's trips back from camp were scarce and Paul had moved in with his girlfriend and lived at the other end of town. Without them, my responsibilities had increased. Not that we ever discussed any of it, but their presence had been a kind of shield and now they had left me alone with Mam without a thought.

Mam seemed pleased I was happy to board. She handed me the Guide to Independent Schools and told me to pick one—a cheap one. I vaguely discerned her reasoning. Keeping an eye on Mam had rendered 'home' less attractive than hanging around on street corners. My school was Catholic, well-mannered and uniformed. The route home promised other delights which now I was twelve, I was busy exploiting. Primarily this new, wild lifestyle meant spending most evenings after school hanging around on street corners and flirting with boys.

Only a few months before I was happy to shut the door on our street. Always on the way home from school, we'd pass a group of big lads from Gotts Park High School. Gotts Park was on the hill opposite our house—closer to the council estate than our Catholic school. We will go on to the Catholic high school and wear uniforms until we are sixteen. But these boys can wear what they want. They have glamour. Each spotty member of the gangly gang wears a combination of Harrington or Ben Sherman jacket, straight-leg stay-pressed trousers and Fred Perry polo shirt. Each item has been carefully chosen in a range of colours from pale chewing-gum grey to charcoal, with the more outlandish members sporting burgundy Doc Martins with yellow laces.

We'd slow down as we approached the boys, stop giggling, lift our chests a little and fix our eyes on the middle distance. We knew that boys in the same uniform as ours might be chased and kicked in honour of ancient inter-school rivalries, so we'd draw a deep breath and be ready to run, just in case. As we came closer, we would be keenly aware of the knot of boys parting to let us through. Their movement threw up whiffs of Old Spice, Denim and stale sweat. We'd do our best to glide past, heads high, dropping each other's hands as we did so. Then, without a word of comment, the boys would be all of a sudden behind us, regrouped in their conversation and us girls would be disappointed without quite knowing why. With no one to show off to, we'd slouch and scuff our soles along the ground, shoulders hunched, and reach once again for each other's hands.

Now these glamorous older lads were my friends, in the distant way boys are friends when you can't actually sit with them or speak to them, but rather hang around the bus stop with your group of girls and throw insults at them instead. I think Mam was getting me away from all this, as well as simply getting me out of the way.

The Guide wasn't much help. I found it very difficult to choose between the schools. Almost every ad featured the school's name across the top of the page in heavy gothic or Roman font, and featured a photo of a country house with a variety of white, healthy-looking children either walking toward or away from the house with a selection of expensive-looking text books under their arms. There wasn't very much to go on.

I decided early that I wanted to go to a mixed school— sitting at the back and laughing with the boys in my class had taken up Mr Hugh's maths lessons for the past three years and I saw no reason why the fun and games should stop when I had established my new court. Other than this, I gauged the uniforms—one home-counties place looked promising but the unholy alliance of yellow and black it forced the kids to wear ruled it out. I, fat and fashion conscious, would not look like a bumble bee for the next four years. Another place featured swimming in an outdoor pool every morning between April and July. I thought wistfully of Mallory Towers for a moment, before deciding that would be living hell for me, the least sporty of anybody I knew.

A few more were too expensive, several were too far away according to Mam ("But you've just passed your driving test," I complained.) So, restricted to a two-hour driving time, fees that were as low as possible and a uniform which wasn't completely hideous, I eventually settled on a small independent in North Yorkshire near Robin Hoods Bay. The school is still there and, besides some new buildings sympathetically constructed in the grounds (which an estate agent would describe as 'extensive') it is essentially as it was when Mam and I turned up in the spring of 1983 in her ancient white Mini, to look around and be interviewed by the principal, Mrs Black.

The journey, it turned out, was to be the first Mam had embarked on of any length since triumphantly passing her driving test at her fourth attempt. She was around 50 then, and as she sat almost frozen behind the wheel staring with wild eyes through the windscreen, my job was to be navigator. This meant trying to tally what the map showed me with the route Paul had worked out for us. The journey of around ninety miles started well. We'd almost made it past York before the first disaster struck. Mam had stopped the car at a roadside café so we could have a cup of tea. She then refused to get back in it.

"I can't do it. I can't get back in the car. I'll have to phone someone to pick us up," she whined, while I stood around in the car park, embarrassed and useless. Then, like the sun breaking through, Mam decided as quickly as she'd given up, that in fact she could go on. I hopped in the car gratefully before she changed her mind. She started the engine, waited until there wasn't so much as a speck of traffic on the horizon, then pulled out cautiously into the road, and we were back on track making our stately progress north.

The coast was still very far however, and it was only another twenty minutes or so before we had another mishap. At each and every junction we passed, I had fallen into the habit of shouting: "Not this one. Go straight on." I had missed one while I was peering at the map, when Mam said "Christ, I've turned left!" and we were all of a sudden on the slip road heading off the motorway in the wrong direction. After persuading her that all she needed to do was carry straight on and re-enter the motorway from the next slip road, we were again, back on our now much longer than expected journey.

All too soon, leaving the safety of the motorway meant we were presented with other problems. Paul's route took us over Devil's Elbow, a famously steep and treacherous stretch of road through the North Yorkshire Moors. The Mini struggled with the gradient. Mam crawled the vehicle up the bank in first gear. I leaned forward and held my breath to help her. The decent into Fylingdales itself was such a glorious relief, and the prospect of another journey like this one so terrible, that I was sold on the school long before I climbed, wobbly-kneed, out of the car, and into a scene of such outrageous beauty I hardly believed that I could be allowed to wander in it, never mind become a part of it.

In front of us, was a grand Georgian manor house with a wonderfully solid, symmetrical appearance. It had a front door with a deep porch supported by half-rounded pillars and flanked on either side by huge bay windows. On the three upper floors, smaller windows echoed those grand bays. Kids ran around us, smartly dressed in grey and carrying books under their arms and jerseys slung over their shoulders, just like in the Guide. A girl wearing what I was soon to learn were jodhpurs led two horses past us and up a track into the woodland while Mam and I were still stood close to the car, gaping.

We were saved when Mrs Black emerged from her smoke-filled office to greet us. Her mother had founded the school in the 1930s, and she was the poshest person I had ever stood close to. I can still clearly remember the shock of her voice. It was high pitched, tremulous and prissily precise, with none of our flat Yorkshire vowels. Blonde-bobbed and small-boned, Mrs Black had been an actress in her youth, and she was now perhaps in her early fifties, but still she radiated a kind of cut-glass glamour that carried the scent of weekend country-house parties and choppy mornings serving glasses of port to the hunt.

Mrs Black's personality sold the school brilliantly—somehow she managed to imply that that the school was a doorway to this lifestyle, despite the fact that once inside the buildings it was clear that they were well and truly battered from the feet and elbows of two hundred children. It was also totally unmodernised. There were flagstone floors, open fires, and a chill wind blowing through every window pane, under every door and down every chimney, and the servant's bells and Agas seemed to date from before civilisation. But it was an easy sell, and Mrs Black sealed the deal by leading us to the back of the manor house, where from a raised terrace overlooking grounds laid out by Knot, the gardens fell away to tennis courts, then woodland, then farmland then the sea, in vista reaching from the beach at Robin Hoods Bay to the cliffs at Ravenscar. It was quickly decided that I would join the school the following term—the summer term. This was only a few weeks away, and if Mrs Black noticed the unseemly rush to get me out of home and away to school as soon as possible, then she didn't betray an iota of surprise.

13.

Monday

I installed the phone next to my bed specifically for days like these. They're the kind of days when it's difficult to leave the comfort of the continental quilt, when phoning in to work sick is a terror, and when even the guilty pleasure of watching *This Morning* can't cheer me up. The phone rings. And rings. I try to ignore it—the make-over victim is due back to show off her new look at 11.04 after Dr Phil has finished dispensing advice of the "go and see your GP" variety to distressed callers. I haven't actually rung in to work yet, but they'll assume. The call might be my boss checking up on me. But if it were a friend I'd like to hear some gossip from the outside world. It might be my best friend ringing with news. I decide to take the chance that it might be of the bad kind.

On the sixth ring, my last chance before the answering machine kicks in, I pick up the receiver and instantly hear my mistake.

"Hello"

"What's the matter? Work told me they think you're ill. What's wrong?"

And I'm trapped. I sigh, quietly. "Nothing, I'm fine, Mam. Stop worrying. I'm fine, honest."

"You sound a bit throaty. Why aren't you at work if you're fine?"

Deep breath.

"I felt a bit ill when I got up. Thought it might be a virus. But I feel fine now. I'm going back in tomorrow. And how are you?"

"There's been another murder, it was all in the paper. A man's helping police with their enquiries."

"That's not very nice."

"He strangled his flat mate then pulled the body around Leeds town centre in a wheelbarrow. He was only arrested when two bystanders stopped to help him get the front wheel up onto the curb. They said they thought that the corpse was a Guy for a bonfire."

"What? In May?"

"Well... I don't suppose they're as clever as you. Anyway, have you got any news?"

"I'm still alive. Other than that, nothing. Have you?"

"Only the murder. Oh, I went to the Post Office this morning and they made a mistake on my savings book. It'll have to be sent away again.

I listen to the air swishing around in the receiver, lost for a response.

"It's very boring being old, Kate."

"I'm sorry they made a mistake on your book Mam, but I'm going to have to go. I'll talk to you tomorrow when I'm feeling better. OK?"

"But you said you already felt better."

"Not quite 100%. Goodbye Mam."

"Bye ..."

But the receiver is already on the hook. I decide I have to get out of the flat. I'm afraid I might actually be as inadequate as my mother makes me feel.

It's a beautiful day. The kind that promises that there *will* be a summer, the sun seems to be encouraging me not to lose faith. Even so, it's lunchtime before I open the living room curtains and three o'clock before I'm finally driven out into the world for milk and fags.

Heading up the street, I walk quickly, head down against the sun, passing ripped and torn fly posters forming abstract paintings on the sooty walls. I use all my attention to pick through the obstacles in my way. Uneven flagstones, cyclists, dog shit, the Telegraph's Appointments section is strewn across the path. A one-armed, rheumy-eyed old man in a baggy piss-stained suit loiters on the corner. I can't help noticing, no matter how hard I try, that he seems to be staring straight through me, rubbing a few coins together in his hand like rosary beads. In my peripheral vision I notice something energetically moving around the front of his trousers. I'm already passed him before I realise it's his other arm.

One of the posters catches my eye and I look up for a minute. The gothic typeface adds a kind of glamour to the abandoned shop fronts, like it's all meant to be. Like a film maker might 'do' this down-at-heel part of London. Of the words on the wall only sections remain "...ew ...ingle out 2 ...ay." Once I start to read them, I can't stop. The activity slows me down even further.

I'm finally forced to stop reading and concentrate on crossing the road. It's a busy route and the pavement judders with the weight of greedy traffic. I can feel the tail wind of an articulated lorry as it speeds through an amber light. I must be too close to the edge of the pavement. The lorry is the starting gun and though I do my best to prevent them my thoughts run ahead of me anyway.

"I'm standing here fine and well now, but how long is it likely to be before I'm lying in mushy pieces on that tarmac? It's not called a bus lane for nothing. It is ten feet to the middle of the road but only five between me and the outside wheel of that lorry. Or is it only a couple of millimetres of artery wall that stands between the driver's heart bursting and his out-of-control vehicle mowing me down here on the pavement?"

It seems that the walk to the paper shop has taken forever. I know that it's about ten minutes from my flat—five if I'm running to get back in time for *Coronation Street*. But today, even the street beneath my feet feels somehow insubstantial, as if it may melt and I go through the sinking tarmac until the black sludge closes over my waist, my handbag, my necklace and finally my head and there is no trace of me left.

This thought starts my brain race again: "How solid is the pavement? How solid *can* it be? Drains, pipes, trains, cable, telephone lines (they might be optical now, but do they still need wire to transmit the light?). And the water table! It's rising isn't it? Is there really anything substantial underneath me now? I might fall down and down like Alice, through the thinning municipal stone. I might drown."

On days like this, the treadmill of these thoughts is my natural home and it is exhausting. On other days it isn't so bad. But I am always aware of the undercurrent roaring under my peace of mind. For instance, if I am waiting for a train, I will have calculated just the precise amount of steps forward I would have to take in order to leave the platform behind. I also try to remain aware of who's behind me at all time (do they look disturbed, violent or both?). But I try to do this without looking to avoid drawing the attention of any potential murderer. On the bus I worry should the driver need to brake suddenly, for is my grip on the seat in front strong enough to stop my sailing through the massive plate-glass windows?

Danger wears so many disguises; it's becoming a full-time job keeping up with them. By the time I get home with my pack of ten, I am a mess of sweat, fear and adrenaline. I have forgotten the milk. The walk up to the shop was clearly a bad idea. Next time, I won't get out of bed at all.

14.
New Girl

It's a bright spring day, and somehow Mam and I have made it back up to North Yorkshire in her little white Mini even with a second-hand metal trunk taking up all of the back seat. Next to it is a baby-sized trunk of about eighteen inches square. This is my tuck box, a kind of hand-luggage and all my most important things are in here: my pencil case, teddy and reading books. My big trunk is full of my clothes—except they aren't my clothes yet, they are the stuff the school has told Mam she must buy me and every single thing is new.

There are blue checked American Pie blouses and blue jeans to wear after school, and grey skirts and shirts together with burgundy school ties and a heavy, boiled wool burgundy blazer for school-time. I have a white airtex shirt and a grey 'divided skirt' for games and, for reasons which are as yet a mystery, a tartan woollen travel rug. I have six pairs of navy knickers, six pairs of white knee socks and every single item has a Cash's name tape sewn in by Mam's own hand. All the clothes are strange and stiff and Mam has made me wear the school-time uniform—skirt, shirt and tie—for the journey, even though it's a Saturday. All of my new life is in that trunk and travelling to meet it I am terrified and excited.

This time, after we drive down the tree-lined road to the grand main school building, the little mini has to jostle for a space to park. The driveway is full of children and their parents unloading bags and trunks, kissing and hugging, generally knowing what to do. Me and Mam are flummoxed again.

'Let's stay here a minute,' she says.

I, taking my hand off the door handle, gratefully agree.

But someone must have seen us: for both of us notice a stolid, grim-faced woman walking toward the car and we are forced out of politeness to abandon our Mini-haven and face this new world.

'You must be Katy. I'm Miss West,' and she smiles at us, but it isn't a face that's used to smiling, so it comes across as a kind of weird contortion, as if she would more willingly go for my neck with bared teeth than open the Mini's passenger door.

"Philippa! Philippa!' Miss West bellows at the hubbub of people as I climb out. A tall, thin, blonde girl appears, and I and my tuckbox are handed over to her like a parcel, while Mam is gently guided towards the office.

'Philippa will show you your dorm. You'll be able to say goodbye later,' grimaces Miss West and I'm unwilling to believe her.

'Are you in second or third year?' Philippa asks me. She seems friendly enough, but like Miss West, she shouts everything rather than just saying it.

'Second.'

'You're in my dorm then. Follow me!'

As we climb first one flight of stairs, then another, and finally, another, I feel increasingly ridiculous. Everyone is wearing jeans with lots of different colourful tops and jumpers. I am trussed up in my shirt and tie like an oven-ready turkey, trying to answer Philippa's questions, carry the tuck box and breathe as I lumber up the endless staircase. The noise is unbelievable: the tatty, wipe-clean surfaces echo with the footsteps and shouts of hundreds of kids, and all the while Philippa lets rip a barrage of questions at ear-splitting volume: "Where was your last school?" she yells. "Why are you joining in the summer term? Nobody joins in the summer term. Were you expelled? Are you going to be in the 'A' group or the 'B' group?" Among the din and interrogation I am aware of the sweat forming in my armpits as I climb and climb. The noisy stairwell takes me further and further away from Mam and the sparse comfort of all that's familiar, while a hundred curious faces peer into mine as they pass.

When we eventually reach the final landing, Philippa opens one of the dark, heavy wooden doors facing us. I walk behind her into a room which is crowded with second-hand looking gear: four metal bunk-beds which could have come off a merchant ship they are so narrow, two enormous chests of drawers which lean slightly, and a sink in front of the bay window. This means there is only a small central space in the room in which to stand. This room is, apparently, already home to seven girls. I will be the eighth, but for now it is as empty of girls as it is full of furniture.

'We're first back,' shouts Philippa. 'That's your bed,' she says, pointing to one of the bottom beds on the bunk nearest the window. I try to fold my large bottom into the bed, finding as I sit down that the mattress barely insulates my buttocks from the slatted springs beneath. I lean back gingerly, struggling to fit my head under the bed bearing down above me.

'Boys up!' someone screams from out in the hall.

'What does that mean?' I quickly ask Philippa, as it's obvious she's about to run out in the direction of the shouting.

She pauses and looks at me as if I'm stupid. 'Boys are up here,' she says, simply, already halfway out of the room. 'They're bringing the trunks up.'

As the door slams thunderously behind her, I place my tuckbox next to my feet. I wonder where my trunk is, where my Mam is. Then from nowhere, an alarm bell goes off. The ear-splitting sound reverberates off the old, bubbly glass in the windows, the tatty lino and the iron bedsteads. Together with the noise, the harsh edges of the room; its thin bare mattresses and gaping, half-open drawers, are shocking. It looked so different when I saw it on our visit: filled as it was with colourful stuff—jumpers, posters, school books, slippers—strewn around by a half-a-dozen girls vying for space.

Just as I decide that I can't stay in the room alone—I feel like a burglar—Philippa remembers me and her head appears from around the door.

'That was the lunch bell,' she says, before her head disappears with another slam that almost sends the door off its hinges.

I am hungry, but I need to find my Mam and that Philippa lass has been no help at all, so I venture out of the room into the corridor. It is in chaos. There are teams of boys hauling heavy trunks up the stairs and, after a quick glance at the instructions on each lid, literally throwing them into various rooms from the doorways. I don't see mine, so I edge past them and their open curiosity until I reach the bottom of the stairs. I am almost back in the hall where we first came in but something stops me before my foot leaves the final step. Mam is stood near the front door with the headmistress.

'Here she is!' cries Mrs Black on seeing me, a little over-enthusiastically I think. I can hear in her voice the slightly over-relieved tone of adults who have settled potentially awkward business, usually financial. But then, I can see Mrs Black is the type to behave as if money was the kind of beastliness she can face only in extremis, rather than, say, something of which she is really rather fond.

Mam is looking a bit excited, a bit shiny-eyed, and I am torn between wanting to hold and comfort her, and wanting to get rid of her as soon as possible. I know that she will be afraid now, having to drive back to Leeds alone. I know, or hope, that she will miss me. But instead of rushing to her, giving her a hug or even a kiss, I do the cowardly thing. I remain at a safe distance from her and Mrs Black, and from where I stand on the bottom step, I offer Mam a quick awkward smile. Then, because this isn't enough, I chance a wave. I daren't look too closely into her face, because she or I might cry, so instead I turn and begin the climb back up to my new home.

15.

Downhill

When you have a broken mind, people always know, no matter how well you think you've hidden the cracks. Today is one of those days when I feel the deep cleft is on show for all to see. It may be a golden, sunny afternoon—if bitter cold—but I walk the street toward Mam's flat with my loneliness attached to my heels, dragging behind like a recently shed skin. I hide behind sunglasses tears which are just on the verge of flowing from red-rimmed sleepless eyes.

If you are lucky enough to suffer only hairline cracks in your personality, with fortune in your favour and, perhaps, with sufficient love, you might never even realise they are there. But if you suffer a deeper fissure, the kind of fault that can rapidly spread from the inside out, so that an imperfection deeply buried makes its way up to the surface and emerges as a crevasse; if you are unlucky enough to carry a crack like this, it may open up at any time and shatter even the most gorgeous carapace, as an inclusion can cause a diamond to shatter like cheap paste.

From calm to crashing pain and crumbling despair,

the personality disintegrates like a melting ice-flow, not in a gradual drip-drip away of reason, but a coruscating series of collapses. Loved ones get to stand uselessly on the sidelines and watch as the pretty facade you have spent years constructing, decades even, falls clean away. It reveals a twitching, bloody mass of scar tissue as the personality who is really in control, like the awful finale to an episode of *Doctor Who*, when the villain's near-human face melts to show the bestial creature lurking inside the machine.

This is one of the worst aspects of my depression: that this individual is the 'real' me. She is ready to reoccupy my mind at the shortest notice, picks a time when the calm, coping woman I pretend to be is feeling a little wobbly. Perhaps I'm a little bit blue, and unwisely take a short break from optimism and purposeful busyness to stupidly indulge in a glass—or bottle—too much of wine, a flick through a photo album, or a CD of old songs. Stepping out for a moment, relaxing for even a short time, taking for granted the peace of mind which others seem to assume by right, can trigger the arrival of black clouds which may take days or weeks or months to disperse.

The invasion of this dark fog makes it hard simply to lift one's legs over the edge of the bed of a morning, because, really, why bother? The fog seems real, the clear skies of a day earlier a mirage. So the fog, paradoxically brings a kind of clarity in its wake. The cheerful person you were yesterday was illusionary. She was a deluded idiot who foolishly forgot that the contented world they inhabited just 24 hours earlier, well, that was as insubstantial as a snowflake.

I now know the truth. I am fat. Actually I am not just fat, I am disgustingly obese. I am not capable of writing the books I have dreamed about; hell I can't even string a sentence together that isn't about me. These beliefs lurk, even after the clouds part, so that one may at any moment thoughtlessly put a foot too close to the edge of the ravine and fall back into the darkness.

This time when Mam sees me at the door, she doesn't shout her hellos or tell me about her chilblains. She doesn't start discussing Monty or Treacle, or ask if I've eaten. What she does is this: she looks at me hard, knitting her eyebrows together so that she looks like Paul. Then she stands aside and allows me into the flat, gingerly, as if I were the new insurance man whom she doesn't yet totally trust. Then she follows my slumped shoulders to the sofa and instead of sitting she silently makes her way into her little kitchen and puts the kettle on. And even in the cavernous silence of misunderstandings which lay between us, her action reassures me that there is one solid fact we can both rely on. It is this: I have come here because I have nowhere else to go.

16.
Withered Blooms

That day I turned up at her door, Mam looked at me and the sight was one she had hoped never to witness again. You see, there's something I haven't told you. When I sought shelter at Mam's little flat, accepted her hot sweet tea, and unpacked my wounded sense of self onto her Argos sofa, it was not the first time she'd seen one of her children broken. While the twelve year-old me was being packed off to boarding school, my brother Paul, the most beauteous of her children, was suffering. I have a picture of him from before I was born. It is of a Paul I never knew. In this photograph he is perhaps ten years old, skinny in a collarless grey jacket and black shorts and squinting up at the camera, foal-like, his appeal all the more precious because fleeting. Everybody who met this Paul loved him: the boy with eyes the colour of lichen bloom.

At the beginning of the 1980s, another Paul, nine years older than me and motorcycle mad, jettisoned any notion of a calm, safe clerical job and set himself up as a motorcycle courier. He had fallen in love with motorbikes after getting his first moped at 16, so couriering was obvious really: it was lucrative, carrying the documents which deal-by-deal built the new economic boom up and down the motorway. And the extra money for taking one job after another was too much to turn down for a boy of twenty, who was anyway a bit anti-social, who probably had no party to attend, no pal to stand at a bar with. When I picture him on his bike he is always alone, nobody riding pillion, nobody at his back.

His own boss, the type who wouldn't listen to pleading, Paul would always go his own way. For instance, in his teens he had stopped eating very much: Mam tried to tempt him with fresh meat, scampi, prawns, treat food in those days. But he ate one thing at a time, sometimes for weeks. Perhaps nothing but crisps for a fortnight, then suddenly, the crisps replaced by digestive biscuits. He passed through this mysterious phase but he remained very thin for the rest of his life: cheeks concave, eyes permanently dulled, the once beautiful child destroyed.

As he matured he became restless, found it difficult to make lasting friends, everything was difficult, uneasy. Moving from job to job, he'd either walk out or get the sack. He was often times a jealous introvert, but in the space of a day or a couple of hours could become a garrulous extrovert. It was difficult to relax in Paul's presence, for it was difficult to know which Paul you'd get. There was something of the thwarted romantic about him, so that his expectations for excitement, for a life lived in colour, were bound always to be found wanting.

When he was sixteen he announced to Mam that he was leaving home to join a travelling fair. He packed his blue duffle bag and off he went. When he came back after two days, it wasn't the first time Mam breathed out with the relief of it, of seeing him return unscathed. But Paul was reduced slightly with every disappointment, with every dream that didn't deliver. That there was something seriously wrong seems obvious now, but it was obscured from us who were closest to him by the drama of the moment. It is this troubled young man I remember most vividly, a lad who was already almost transparent with anxiety even though he was yet to meet the greatest challenges of his life. The gorgeous and curious child in the photo is a boy I never knew.

One wet night, he accepted a couriering run from Leeds to London and back. This was one of the most profitable jobs he could be offered, and though he had already been riding all day he thought he could handle the 400-mile round trip and sleep later. Inevitably he was wrong. He fell asleep while riding his bike up the M1 and crossed the central reservation into oncoming traffic. In the crash he suffered serious internal injuries and almost lost his left leg. My brother endured eighteen months of hospitalisations and around a dozen surgeries to save it. Innovative doctors managed to remove a muscle from his back and use this to replace the part of his calf which had been ripped away in the impact. But it was a year and a half of bodily smells barely hidden by antiseptic, of scant privacy, of ward companions coming and going, of orange squash in plastic cups, and of course, of pain.

But still nobody thought to look beneath the flesh at what impact the hood of that car, the face of that startled driver, had had on his mind. He still had spirit, a skewed idealism that made him think he could make anything happen. In hospital in Sheffield he went on hunger strike to force his transfer to Leeds, and transferred to Leeds he was. Stuck at home on crutches, lonely and isolated from his beloved motorbikes, he was featured in our local paper. Under the headline 'Penpal plea from Paul, the pot-leg prisoner' he asked for people to write to him. And they did. So while he endured the slow recovery from his injuries, he began to write to a woman, Mary. Mary would eventually become his wife. Her appearance was a hope, a promise that everything would be alright. That after all, Paul's life would be like a journey that begins badly, with panic and worry and missed connections, but once on its way settles into a pleasant predictability. But Mam had exhaled too soon. The marriage would last only a short time.

17.
Miss Cellophane

I am sat on Mam's sofa, serene and fat like a brown Buddha. It is only a couple of days since I, bedraggled, turned up on her doorstep. The black dog of despair is still with me, but the bitch is becalmed by food from my mother's kitchen. All our old favourites have been paraded before my ever-ravenous eyes. Raspberries and ice cream, roast potatoes, crunchy-skinned chicken, slick brown gravy, fine beans, crumble and homemade sponges. Mam is feeding me back to life.

She has not asked me why I am here, and now, after a couple of days, I am glad. I have thought and thought about it, but still wouldn't be able to give her a convincing answer even if she dared venture the question. Is it a broken heart? An obvious conclusion, but as she knows my heart is already in pieces it wouldn't occur to her that further damage could cause this extraordinary visit, my extraordinary collapse. Yes, there was an unsatisfactory relationship, because there always was. I had not learned that love is chimera: the harder I chased it, tried to bring it into view, the more it changed shape, slipped my grasp.

Because of my obsessive scrutiny, my suspicion that they may be internally flawed, I had made my relationships into broken clocks and gleefully reduced them to their parts. Spreading them out on the kitchen table, fascinated with the possibility in those shiny nuts and wheels, I always realised too late that there was no hope of reassembling them, turning them back into something of purpose.

I am beginning to look at Mam with new eyes. When I arrived at her door, face bloated with tears and pain, she hadn't known what to do with me. We waited in silence while she made the tea, then stuck her head in the fridge to find something, anything not too elderly, for us to eat. Eventually we made our way to the sofas, each waiting for the other to set the tone for how this unplanned stretch of time together should be managed. I sat in the kettle-steam and cat hair and pondered the possibility of successful improvisation, but also the dangers of a mistimed tale or off-key comment. As the silence grew more oppressive I was the one who, as usual, cracked first.

"Aren't you going to ask me why I'm here?"

I shouted at her, thinking I had no fear left, believing that the pain made me brave.

But then she looked at me full in face, and her blue eyes turned brimstony.

"Well, what do you want me to say? You turn up here, with your long face....."

But she allowed the scold to fade on her lips because fat tears began rolling down my fat cheeks. Instead, she looked away from me, embarrassed.

It was soon after this that she began to cook. I had found my mother's table, and if she remained something of a chimera herself, I didn't mind. I was fairly numb to her disinterest, even found it soothing, and the bustle of her cooking became a calming backdrop to the chaos inside. And her cooking remained excellent, even if the food was softer now, and took her longer than it used to and bending down to the oven had become a creaking chore.

Our silences remained hardly broken by a succession of sensual tastes. One after another, now the slick of sweet-creaminess presses against the roof of my mouth as another dessert is demolished, now the tart bite of lemon anoints the oily crack of a fork forced into battered fish. From doing absolutely nothing, merely lying, breathing, wishing for escape from this body, I actively *ate* and savoured, rather than forced down, her foodstuffs. Anticipation returned: I looked forward to delicious-smelling scones coming out of the oven. So that waiting for those scones in a damp fug of pastry fumes, I could already taste their delicious buttery baptism.

But even the silence couldn't last, and as so often it was an exterior force which ended our companionable, if gluttonous truce. That force was *Antiques Roadshow*.

On the telly, a woman about my mother's age

unwrapped a doll. It was scruffy, dressed in pre-war fashions and had a face that had clearly once been shiny but was now cracked and filthy.

"I had one of those," Mam says. "It's a cellophane doll. A little girl on the boat pushed her face in. They were cheap even then."

I was startled by this nugget of truth, or perhaps in my misery I was shocked to see her as a person, with a past, a history of her own. I had long regarded her as a terrifying source of shame. Now during these convalescent days, exhausted by the formless terrors which haunted my waking hours, I had lost all sense of her at all. She had become merely food and tea. But this was new: a story about a cellophane doll.

And this was how it began. This is how my mother gave her story to me, through the slow unwrapping of a cellophane doll in a cloche hat, a long overdue plaything lost out of its time.

18.
Boarding

I was not settling in to the new school regime. The trouble started early. During my first term, I was outraged to have been assigned to the 'B' group. Each form year comprised two classes: an 'A' group and a 'B' group, with the first being brighter and shinier, and the second consisting of those who, if fortunate, were good at a sport, or at least good-looking. I was horrified—the idea of not being selected for the top set outraged me. And as I was neither pretty nor athletic, I urgently set about showing the school exactly who they were dealing with. I immediately began to study hard to catch up on the two terms of work I'd missed. This was just as well as it was already obvious I didn't fit in. I did however recognise that there was much I could learn. Most of my seven dorm-mates were the children of forces personnel posted abroad, and by no means all were of officer class. I was relieved that they seemed fairly normal: one or two even went slightly out of their way to be friendly.

Philippa continued to show me the ropes that first week. "Don't talk to her" she pointed at one unfortunate day girl, as we stood in the school hall, called The Barn after its original purpose, for assembly.

"Why not?"

"Because nobody will talk to *you* if you do!" was Philippa's no nonsense response. I would have made my life at school much easier for myself if I'd listened to her. Instead I courted unpopularity by not caring if I stood out. I had always stood out—in my Catholic comprehensive school where Chris Latte and I were the only two children in the form who weren't white, and on our street in Leeds, where everyone knew me as Mrs Massey's little coloured girl. Why should I not stand out here?

At first, the time passed in a whirl of learning to respond to the bell which rang constantly from 8am when it roused us from our narrow spindly bunk beds, to 8pm when it signalled the end of the day. At 8.30am the bell rang for breakfast, at 9.30 it rang for assembly, at 12.30 it rang for lunch and at 2 it rang for the start of afternoon lessons. In between mealtimes it rang every hour as a signal for us to change classrooms. Life, it seemed, was to be a succession of bells. And queues. Queues for everything: tea, bread, laundry, toiletries, tuck, pocket money, everything that was available to us, cost the price of waiting in an orderly line. It sensibly kept us busy, but I was a spoilt child, unused to waiting. Here, in this new place of hard, easy-clean surfaces, where there was no privacy even in the bathroom, and where I was expected to take my turn washing up among other chores around the school, here I received neither indulgence from my carers and nor was I rewarded with power, as this was reserved for older pupils, the seniors. It hurt that I had none of the power I enjoyed at home. It hurt a lot.

My lack of friends, as well as adjusting to life within an institution meant that, even with the system of bells keeping us busy, I still spent hours and hours alone. My solution was to pretty much ignore my predicament and fall back on my brain. I took to sitting on my small wooden tuck box in the corner of the dorm with my head down, desperately fighting through *Ecco Romanus*, my first Latin textbook. I had completely failed to see how important it was to conform in this tight-knit little society, and had immediately set myself up as a threat to their norms. Most damagingly, at the end of that first term I got the best marks out of the B group students, thereby stealing the (cash!) prize for this achievement from several of my classmates who had worked hard all year competing for the honour.

If it weren't enough that I was stealing the prizes from under their noses, I decided to go on hunger strike as well. After ten days or so with very little food, I eventually fainted in church, and so finally got the attention I craved. Someone on the staff must have telephoned Mam because she drove up to visit me. But while I was overjoyed to see her, she was clearly less than thrilled to have to make the journey over the North Yorkshire moors twice in under two months.

She picked me up from school in her little Mini and drove us away from the stoney downpour-soaked buildings as if we were really free. We drove down into Robin Hood's Bay and sat in her car as the wind conspired with the grey North Sea and the downpour to render the view from the windows invisible. The intimacy of just sitting there was what I needed. Mam predictably told me that I'd wanted to go to school, it was too late to bail out now, etc. etc. During her tight-lipped tirade, I sat and enjoyed the focus of one person on me, just me. One person who wasn't a stranger. After being reassured that I was still who I thought I was and hadn't disappeared into the crowd of pupils, as I was perhaps required to do, I calmed down slightly. But perhaps I was learning. Sat in my Mam's ancient white mini sheltering from the driving rain, I realised that after all that effort, after starving myself and blackmailing my mother until I got what I wanted, there was actually nowhere else for me to go.

I had endured one term at this foreign school, and that had been in summer. By the time the new school year started in the chilly September I was keen never to return to the place again. But of course I had to see it through, Mam made that clear. Her investment in my uniform had been substantial and it wasn't going to waste and, though I was unaware of it then, she had plans afoot to scale the heights in her new profession and I was simply not going to get in the way, eating or no. And in truth, even with the bells, the lessons and the lack of privacy, underneath all my misery and moaning I knew that this place of learning, of longing, was still better than being at home.

19.

I Vow to Thee

While I struggled to adjust to school life, and Paul simply struggled, our fragile family suffered yet another assault, this time from outside forces. At about the time I was tearfully unpacking my trunk and hoping that someone, anyone, would talk to me, President Gaultiere's Argentine troops invaded and captured the Falkland Islands. Stranded on the North Yorkshire Moors, events in the outside world lost meaning, and the first I heard of the war came in a letter from Mam.

I had no idea that the country had been convulsed by a kind of ecstatic jingoism, or that our first lady Prime Minister was driven by a deadly determination to prove she had balls. Union flags were waved, young lads, our bravest and best, sailed thousands of miles away, becoming smaller and more indistinct as the distance between them and their loved ones grew, until, at last they were no longer individuals but part of a body of men, a task force, a bloody machine. "Since the humiliation of Suez, Britain has needed to prove she can persecute a successful campaign abroad," I remember some white-haired chap opining on the telly. I had no idea what he was talking about, but I caught the chip on his shoulder, and experienced for the first time the dangerous marriage of grievance with a kind of natural, assumed authority. Could it be that the country actually looked forward to all this?

At first the conflict simply passed me by. At school, it was accepted that our breakfast of cereal and door-steps of bread which we ate at long wooden tables in the sparely-decorated dining hall would be accompanied by the quiet crying of homesick new arrivals, not the radio and the news. It didn't always begin quietly, but sounds of distress that rose above a snuffled whimpering were soon stamped on by dining companions. "Stop beefing Massey!" a senior girl shouted from across the room, this was enough to quell my louder sobs. And then, one ordinarily miserable morning, I had more reason for tears than usual: Mam's usual letter informed me that on Andrew had left with his Parachute regiment to sail to the Falklands on the liner *QE2*. I had little idea of what this actually meant, except that now I had gone and Andrew had left the country, there was only Paul to look out for Mam, and I was certain it was too tough a task for him alone.

I could do little for my brother at the other end of the world. From the perspective of the far-off North Yorkshire Moors, the war seemed to drag and drag. I saw what news reports I could, I began to read the daily newspapers the school bought in for its pupils. The news showed an injured soldier being carried on a make-shift looking stretcher. His cries of agony were unbounded, brutal. He waved a bloody stump where the lower part of one of his legs used to be. I was terrified for my brother.

I have a letter he posted back from the islands. I must have written to him pouring out my woes, typically and shamefully without a thought of what he might be going through. His reply was full of the love I had long since taken for granted.

"Glad to receive a letter from you," he wrote. Before mobile phones and email, letters were all he had, but then Andrew has never been one for overstatement. "Shame you have not settled in yet but give it time. In the end when you're in a top job getting thousands a year and the people who mock you are working for peanuts, then you can laugh at them. Always, as your teachers say, stay proud. The main thing is that you enjoy yourself, making the most of the opportunities you have. When anyone mocks you or calls you black just answer them mildly ("Yes, I am black"). A mild answer turns away rage. I should not be here too long now. Will come up to see you as soon as I can. Will certainly come up to see Mam as she has been so good to me. I reckon we have a mum in a million."

I am not alone in believing that the big brother I had then was the best big brother in the world. It is a fantasy of every little sister that theirs is special, that theirs is extraordinary, and I was and to some extent still am, no different. But always with my family where there is a particular expression of love there is the shadow of a new horror lurking somewhere close behind.

He signed off "Thinking of you always"—as I believe he was. But I doubt he was thinking of a twelve-year-old, rather he thought of a strangely old soul. I was ridiculously proud of him, and proud of his sacrifice, but was I proud of my country? It is a question I've thought about often since Andrew went to war: it was the first time I had thought about a larger social unit than me, Mam, Andrew and Paul. There was this thing, this country, a nation, and my brother might die for it.

20.

Municipal Grass

While I am still proud of my brother and admire his courageous optimism, in truth I cannot enjoy an uncomplicated affection for a place where I am paid to use my intellect, but am more admired for my exotic looks. Where I have been spat on in the street and am routinely ignored in smart shops, where I am anyway more likely to be followed by a security guard than a helpful assistant. My difference has excluded me from a closer relationship with the land of my birth, a relationship that I am aware other people take for granted. An event from my childhood illustrates that this exclusion is not specific to me, but rather one which is the result of being exposed to the worst as well as the best of my birth nation.

One day when I was playing out on a scrubby bit of grass which we called 'down the park', a stranger, a woman, approached me. She looked at me hard with beautiful, almond-shaped eyes the colour of soot and asked: "Are you Egyptian?". Her mouth smiled, but those eyes were pools of misery. I so much wanted to comfort her that I paused before answering. I could see how lonely she was. She carried her loneliness with her, like a shadow or a shedding skin. I realised that to lie, even if it were for the best reasons, wasn't possible, so I told the truth. "No" I said, and, embarrassed at her exposed emotions, I couldn't meet her eye and carried on playing as if she wasn't there. Very soon she wasn't.

This event stayed with me because now I think I know why this woman was so sad. It could have been simple homesickness, that she just wanted to talk about her country with someone who understood. But with only the evidence of unreliable memory to go on, I think that for her, her sense of self must have been defined by her country of origin. Not her race, or religion, but that politically-expedient unit of organisation: her nation. This idea was so important to this woman that, without someone to share her memories with—even someone so tangential, a stranger and a child—she was effectively missing some part of herself.

So my love for this country is pragmatic, not the romantic love of the truly patriotic which of course exists partly on the level of myth. People ask 'Where are you from?' and I worry less about how to answer, than the possibility that I have no answer. I cope well enough within the skin I have been given, but I am aware of its ramifications too. Being of many worlds, and none, the product of two or three cultures but nowhere decisive, means much more than simply having a different appearance. It involves a negotiation which excludes me from a deep attachment to a single nation or culture, an attachment that so many people around me enjoy, or simply do not realise how much a part of them it is until they are ripped from it, like the sad-eyed woman who I have never forgotten who'd hoped that she'd found a missing part of herself playing on that scrubby bit of grass.

21.

Omerta

Lying on her sofa, I now see that Mam's visit to the school had sealed something between us. The month or two I had spent boarding was too complex for me, and too alien to her, for me to properly explain why I had stopped eating. And anyway, my appetite returned the moment she left, so there was no need for further discussion.

Today, I would say that I was trying to claw back some control. Before boarding I had pretty much pleased myself: Mam was busy selling herself, the boys had their own grown-up lives and I'd had too much freedom. Too much freedom and too much power. Now I had to move in time with hundreds of other kids, adopt their rhythm. I hadn't realised that I had obviously failed to do this, that I had been thrown in a barrel with a load of other fish and decided to swim in the opposite direction. Somehow I had failed to notice their piscine, contemptuous faces rushing head-on at me. Since I'd learned the nature of Mam's little cottage industry, a wall had grown up between us made up of all the things we couldn't talk about. Time added layers of brickwork, so that by the time we were sat in her Mini, watching the North Sea rain, I couldn't think of a way to explain my situation: there was nothing to say. I was at the threshold of having my own life, and hers, well, that was her business.

But now she'd produced the cellophane doll, a toy from when she was little and unknown to me, a toy that she had loved. And I am again in foreign waters. I am unable to read what this confidence means, but I am too weak to try and decipher it. I am the ideal audience of one.

22.

HMS *Mauritania*

Mam is telling me of a time when she was not my Mam, but Little Yvette. And on the day she is telling me about, Little Yvette sits in the crook of her Daddy's arm, staring down at a sea of hats.

I already know some of this story: Mam's parents had come to England from their home in Canada in about 1936. The Great Depression had bitten deep into the country, but both were pragmatists. Mam's father could cut, polish or construct virtually anything mineral. Mam's mother could kill, cook and preserve virtually anything animal or vegetable. But even two as practical as they could see that the clever money was waiting the depression out in England, where the summers are short and wet, but the winters not so long or harsh.

My grandfather, Horace Massey, met Yvette Ernestine Yolande Gregoire in Quebec when he was tiling a rich man's kitchen. Horace was 28 years old, short, well-built, with a round face and a ruddy complexion. His pale blue eyes bulged slightly but kindly beneath sparse mousy hair. Granny Yvette was working at the house as a maid. She was 18, small and plump and wore her hair in perfect Marcel-waved rivulets. As this hairstyle made clear, she hadn't come from a family who expected to spend their working lives in service. The job was a practical choice: she was working in this wealthy Jewish household to learn English, her life up until that point having been lived entirely among her French-speaking ardently Catholic family in the outlands of the province.

Horace had come to this freezing landscape driven by a sense of adventure. He was a young man, skilled, and had spent nine years in the RAF making it up the ranks to flight sergeant. His first choice for his quest had been New Zealand, but he found out the ticket to the other side of the world cost £20 and he had nowhere near enough money, so Canada had been his second sensible choice.

My grandfather didn't speak French and granny's command of English was poor, but in that genteel kosher kitchen, he kissed Yvette among the broken splinters of tiles. They married less than three months later and set up home in a small wooden house built on stilts so in that in the winter it looked like an oasis in the snow.

But work began to dry up for Horace: people had no money to build anything with, had no money to pay him to fix anything. So the little family will soon leave the wooden house where my mother was born and make the slow journey by sea to seek out Horace's relatives. Eventually, they will arrive in Huddersfield and take their first faltering steps to building a life together in the heat and industry of the industrial north. Horace's sister Grace will be pleased to see them. She is making a living from renting out rooms to families just such as they, though most are streaming in from Europe, not Canada.

Beneath her down-to-brass-tacks, salt-of-the-earth persona Grace is a tragic and mysterious woman. She was made a widow back in the 20s when her husband, a promising boxer known on the circuit as Spider Buck, decided late one night to lay his head on the railway line. Ostensibly, he chose to end his life because his promising boxing career had stalled. This sadness was married with a deep and morbid fear of going down the pit, as nearly every other man he knew did daily. But as ever with my family, I suspect there was more to it than that. Why else would Grace, now a lone widow with two young children to support, have been booed by the mourners at Spider's funeral?

So it is toward mysterious Grace and this unknown country of England that my Mam will soon be journeying. She will leave the little wooden house she stands in front of in one of the few photographs I have of her as an infant. She is about three years old, gorgeous and chubby cheeked. She stands squinting, mid-giggle, into the winter sunshine with no hint of fear.

Through Mam's own eyes, she is telling me about the voyage from Canada to England.

"My father is holding me up so I can see over the

deck rail. Everyone is shouting and waving at us, even people we don't know. There is a celebration and it's because the boat is leaving and we are on the boat along with a lot of other people. But I am confused; if this is a party a lot of the people crushed up against the rail don't look very happy: nearly all of the women are crying. But I am looking down at the people on the shore, they are all tiny and individuals are difficult to make out. Their waving hands sway like corn above wool-covered heads but I can't see my auntie, though I guess she will be crying too.

Daddy points to the box he placed in my hands a moment ago. 'Throw the streamers to the people, Little Yvette' he tells me, and I look at the multi-coloured roles of paper nestled in my box. They are very pretty, like a rainbow, prettier even than Clara, my cellophane doll, and if I throw them over the rail, down and down into the mess of folk below, it is difficult to see how I'll get them back again.

'No!' I shout at him and push my face into the scratchy fabric of Daddy's overcoat. I will not throw my lovely coloured papers away. Daddy and Mammy laugh at me, but Mammy laughs while dabbing her eyes with her best white handkerchief, the one with lace around the edges and a blue 'Y' embroidered on it."

The journey to the ship was a long one and by the time the little family have to say goodbye to their lives in Canada, Little Yvette is very tired. First, they visited granny in Quebec and during the train journey Little Yvette had desperately wanted to wee-wee, but there wasn't a toilet on their train, so she had cried all the way. Then she saw Granny: she had her glasses on and Little Yvette was afraid. She'd never seen the thick glass discs before and they made Granny look like a squirrel, with her eyes all big. Little Yvette screamed when she saw her, and fled to the toilet, which anyway she had been looking forward to seeing far more than Granny.

Listening to Mam talk like this, in full flight, carried by a wind of words, I have felt the sea spray freeze on my face and the relief of that longed-for piss. Mam in full-flow can tell a story so well that you feel like you're in the memory with her. This is just as well, because even with the unending flow of food, I'd rather be anywhere else but here—marooned on Mam's couch sniffing and coughing because Monty keeps trying to sit on me. Yet I find I am drawn into Mam's story even though inside I am screaming for a way out. The breaking of our long silence has been resolved in her favour: she won't listen to me—I must listen to her. But as if acknowledging this she has upped her game: I have never known her so lost in a tale, so vivid on the details, so animated in its delivery.

Instead of the old woman in front of me, I see Little Yvette, standing on the deck with her parents, the last she saw of the sea until the little family arrived in Southampton a week later. In the bowels of the ship, her mummy, Big Yvette, was sick often into the little sink in the corner of their cabin. Only Daddy didn't seem to feel the pitch and toss of the Atlantic. He woke up with them, but then he got dressed and went to the dining deck to eat. Later, he would return to the cabin, now rich with the stench of vomit and resentment, to tell them what he had seen.

The dining room is beautiful, Daddy tells his sick little family, each mahogany bent-wood chair placed at a table setting of silver and crystal. And you can eat as much as you like! Horace's big blue eyes shine at the thought. When he roamed the deck for exercise the sea crashing against the side of the ship was spectacular he reports, and their fellow passengers are fascinating, each has a story to tell. Both the Yvettes listen to him as they rolled fitfully from one side of their tiny bunks to the other, trying but failing to find relief from the nausea which struck them as soon as soon as the boat left dock.

Stuck for an interminable week in the rolling world her parents had brought her to, Little Yvette looked forward to the end of the journey. She wanted the sickness to be over and to arrive in Southampton, which is in England, and where Little Yvette would meet her father's family and Big Yvette would meet her husband's family for the first time before starting a new life in a country where she barely spoke the language.

Watching Mam now, bent and swollen at the joints, you would think she was still that little girl, she is in the moment, doing all the voices, and her performance betrays no hint that she already knows what life this journey will bring her to. Trapped on the sofa, and furious about this ill-considered flow of information, this breaking of our unspoken code of silence, I nevertheless feel myself softening. As Mam continues with her story, I can't help but picture her as that little girl in the photograph, the little girl who squints into the sun, and my heart breaks for her innocence.

23.
Bully

And at this early point in my school career, the serious bullying hadn't yet begun. The girls I had moved in with—the same girls who, over the next three years were to become the closest thing to sisters I ever knew—were just picking on me in a perfunctory sort of way. It was not particularly malicious—they were saving that—but it was focussed and relentless. I couldn't seem to do anything right. In particular, they said I stared at them—I am not sure why or how it emerged that I was a starer, as I didn't recognise myself at all in their accusations—but perhaps I was merely dazed.

One afternoon, I was taking a bowl half-full of rice pudding into the kitchen when Ellen Right walked toward me, widened her eyes, and stared into my face. I snapped and swung the bowl toward her head. It broke, I ran away and Ellen stood holding her head as the blood dripped through her fingers. It turned out she needed three stitches. I hid in the woods until I was ready to face people. The staff, surprisingly, weren't too bad about it, I don't know why I wasn't expelled, but I think it may have been obvious that I wanted out of school, so what better way to frustrate me than by refusing to? Or perhaps it was Ellen's mother's reaction ('Well, she shouldn't have called her names'). Or perhaps the school just needed the money. Just before I had arrived there were two scandals which must have impacted on the bottom line.

The first was the detainment at Her Majesty's Pleasure of a teacher at the school, Graham Smith, for the murder of his French wife, Odette and her lover. The second was, for us girls, far more interesting. Almost the moment I arrived I was told about four fifth-form girls who'd been 'asked to leave'—a milder form of expulsion—just the term before. The unfortunates were caught 'down Bay' getting up to no good with some 'Bay boys'. They had, in actual fact committed two crimes: having sex with non-pupils (there was plenty of sexual activity going on between pupils to which a blind eye was turned) and, more crucially, getting caught in such a compromising position that it was impossible for the school to ignore it. Half the student body were day pupils from the surrounding towns and villages—the day-parents would have expected the school to be seen to take action.

As the Autumn term continued the slow crawl toward Christmas, I was cold all the time. Our dorm was heated by a single hot water pipe which ran around one half of the walls. I regularly peeled frozen socks and knickers I had washed off the dorm window, underwear I had optimistically hung up to dry, not freeze. Also, I continued to put on weight, chiefly by avoiding all forms of physical exercise. I would stand uselessly on the hockey pitch, my body appearing almost entirely spherical because of the layers of clothing I wore. I never smiled, thus ensuring the few team mates who came near soon became as miserable as me. On the odd occasion when the ball came toward me by accident, or God forbid someone was stupid enough to try and pass it to me, I would run in the opposite direction, sometimes even screaming.

This is not quite as pathetic as it sounds. Hockey was brutal, with our PE mistress being the most aggressive player of all. She was famous for her physical courage. On one occasion she was hit in the face during one particularly competitive game. The blow gashed her forehead open and despite the bloody mess her face was in, she walked back up to the school, stood in front of the medical-room mirror and stitched up the wound herself. After one year of hockey hell, I and half a dozen other refuseniks were sent euphemistically to 'pick brambles' on a Wednesday afternoon. This instruction, we understood, roughly translated to: "we don't care what you do, just don't get caught". Actually, yomping about the deserted grounds, having the freedom of the woods, while almost everybody was busy on the games pitches became the highlight of my week.

In fact, the school's remote position afforded us more physical freedom than I think was normal for boarders— we were pretty much free to wander as we liked over the moors and through the woods. As I found the lack of privacy one of the hardest things to bear, I continued to seek out my own company as much as I could. There was a walled rose garden that, though technically off-limits, would prove something of a haven on warm summer evenings when I'd sit on a bench, smoke and watch the espaliered trees until it was time for bed.

The school did what it could to provide other entertainment. It was school legend that Mrs Black once had a speaking part in the *Lavender Hill Mob*, and this fact was used to explain its regular appearance as our Saturday night film. The weekly film was projected onto the wall of the old barn which stood in as the school assembly hall, theatre and gym. Films had to be stopped frequently when a reel needed changing, or the projector overheated. Attending Saturday night films was compulsory. On the upside, the tuck shop was opened half an hour before the movies started, so we tolerated a very strange selection of movies, because we could chomp our way through them high on sugary delights. Comforting a dorm full of traumatized eight year olds after *The Elephant Man*, is a particularly sharp memory, as is sitting through a long black and white movie about an unfortunate farmer's daughter-type girl and an even more unfortunate donkey which got blown up in the end (this may have been *Au Hasard Balthazar*, 1966, by Robert Bresson but I cannot be sure).

It was also during my second term, and my first

experience of what winter was in rural North Yorkshire, that the serious bullying kicked in. I don't know precisely what started it. Was it braining Ellen? Or was it the lavish tuck parcelled up and posted to me by Mam, which I sold to my fellow pupils on credit?

I would write down who owed me how much in very precise columns in a school exercise book. Every Saturday morning, with notebook in hand, I would wait for them outside the sixth form common room where we collected our pocket money. (In my defence, I never once charged them interest, even the miscreants who avoided me on Saturdays, whom I had to chase all week for payment.) Or perhaps it was that the overweight, brown girl from a Leeds comprehensive had been elevated to the 'A' group where I settled comfortably into doing well without much effort.

Or again, maybe it was my butch posing. I was a tomboy who wrestled the boys and thought little of the other girls' attempts to attract their attention. They, of course, couldn't understand why the boys were fascinated by this plump little brown fighter, who wasn't scared of anyone and made out like she didn't care what anyone thought. If fascination was what I had sought, I would have found it fairly easy to attract attention despite my physical disadvantages. I already knew how to do *it*; I just wasn't interested in the *job*. A bit of snogging aside, sex would remain a closed book to me until long after I left the school. It may have been the overexposure, the loss of mystery that occurred when sex was revealed to me, not as a freedom, not as pleasure and certainly not as an expression of love but as a *business*.

So, on top of a lack of interest in sex—the carefully thumbed paperbacks of *Lace* and *Scruples* which were passed from bunk to bunk didn't interest me, the obsessive talk of who-fancies-who left me cold—just about everything I did demonstrated my contempt for the values of the girls around me. And worse, I was making a pretty penny on the side out of them too. They reacted as children still do: by psychologically torturing me until I couldn't take it anymore. This they did by constant reference to 'niggers' being 'dirty'—so now I was a dirty, staring nigger. At one stage the most dominant girl in the dorm, Maddie Dimms, physically elbowed me out of the way of our single mirror. I snapped and, breaking Andrew's injunction to be 'mild', shouted:

"Who do you think you are to push me out of the way? What gives you right?"

She smiled sweetly through the glass at me and replied lightly:

"Just *one* thing, I'm white."

Without breaking her cool she turned and left, trailing behind her two giggling girls.

I would love to recount to you a tale whereby, through a combination of fiendish cunning and goodness of heart, I somehow managed to win over my roommates while exposing their racism. In this version, I would engineer an ending featuring group hugs and tearful apologies. This didn't happen. Instead, I grassed them up, putting the whole sorry story into a letter to Mam. Then I hunkered down on my tuckbox lid, *Ecco Romanus* in hand, and waited.

24.

Reginald Terrace

Mam is still talking. My resentment dissipated a little by her sparkle, I am rapt as I learn how her little family—Big Yvette, Little Yvette and Horace—arrived in England with 25 shillings to their name. First they stayed with Auntie Grace on Trinity Street, Huddersfield. Gracie ran a guest house, but Yorkshire was squalid to Big Yvette's eyes. To her, the shawls, clogs and black-lead fireplaces marked it out as a poor place; one at least ten years behind the Canadian home she'd left behind, where central heating, sheepskin boots and overcoats were the norm.

But she soon had bigger worries, her belly was already swelling with another baby, Little Yvette's little brother, so the family left Auntie Grace's and moved to Horace's home town, Leeds. They lived in a single room with a curtain dividing the sleeping and living areas before they saved enough to rent their own large property in Reginald Terrace where Yvette's little brother was born. Little Yvette wasn't happy about the new arrival, but was comforted by the fact that he was very fat, and anyway she was still the apple of her daddy's eye.

While Horace went out to work, Granny took Little Yvette to the sale rooms behind Leeds railway station to buy furniture for the upstairs rooms at Reginald Terrace, which they intended to rent out. They would charge 16 shillings a week and the rent from lodgers would cover the rent for the whole house. In 1936 there was a glut of people looking for cheap, decent accommodation and the house was in Chapeltown, the then centre of the city's Jewish community.

First, Mr and Mrs Hermann took the tiny box room, the cheapest accommodation in the house. Mr Hermann had been a German officer in the Great War, and they had left Germany because it looked likely Mr Hermann would have to fight again. The Hermanns had been wealthy and told everyone they owned a shop in Germany as grand as Marshall and Snelgrove's in Leeds centre. All that remained of their fortune was a few rolls of cloth they had brought with them. Mrs Hermann would sit all day and sew beautiful, intricate, needlework to sell to the city's finest shops. She even made everyone in the house warm nighties entirely by hand. In a few short years, these garments would be kept by their bedroom doors, kept as a comfort for when the air raid warning shouted, and the whole house decamped to the cellar.

Next door to the Hermann's, an elderly Austrian

woman shared a room with her beautiful daughter, Trudy. Trudy was popular and invited to parties Little Yvette was far too young to attend. One night Little Yvette awoke and lay in her bed listening to strange but energetic music coming through the floor from the Austrians' room. The balalaika Little Yvette heard was played by a handsome Russian émigré, who soon after married Trudy and took her glamorous presence away with him.

Trudy's place was taken by Mrs Reece, who had been living with a Jewish pilot before she moved into Reginald Terrace. However, shortly after her arrival, she informed the other members of the household that, going forward, she wished to be known as Mrs Nardle. Mr Nardle, whoever he was, never came to the house so the name-change was a mystery, but Mrs Nardle was a very feminine woman who had lots of suitors. Perhaps Mr Nardle was one of these men, a man who enjoyed the flamboyant ribbon bows she sewed onto the negligees she swanked around the house in all day. The glamour was perhaps a kind of compensation, because Mrs Nardle was also entirely bald. Every night she applied bright blue ointment to her shiny scalp, and each week, she gave Little Yvette half a crown to take her wig into town to be styled.

Above Mrs Nardle, Dr Austerlitz, a Jewish Austrian doctor of chemistry, lived in the two attic rooms. Like the rest of the tenants, he had fled Europe, but he was also a doctor and duly respected as such. He had, after all, written books. In this household it seemed everybody tried to get on, nobody asked questions about the recent past. No one asked what had happened to Trudy's father. No one demanded of Herr Hermann why he wasn't fit to fight for his country. And if the strings of harmony that bound the strange household together were occasionally a little strained, Little Yvette knew nothing of it.

25.
Duffield

I am telling you my mother's story as she told it to me: straight, with no commentary or embellishment. As I listen, I struggle to make sense of what she is saying, or rather, why she is saying it. Then I realise: my role is not to interpret, to try and work out what her story means for me, it is simply to witness, to accept. Nevertheless, there are episodes where I cannot help but overlay my own meaning, even where she, who's story it is after all, demurs.

Mrs Duffield arrived at Reginald Terrace with a large cage covered with a blanket. Little Yvette was immediately intrigued and Mrs Duffield was happy to have a little girl fall in love with her only companion, a green, partly bald and bad-tempered parrot. It became clear that the parrot and Mrs Duffield endured a fractious relationship. The parrot would shout and swear at her: "Get out of fucking bed!" it would scream. And if in company, Mrs Duffield would quiet it by throwing a cushion at the cage and frightening the bird into silence.

"Who taught it speak like that?" asked Little Yvette.

"The window cleaner at my last place," replied Mrs Duffield.

Little Yvette was fascinated and repelled by the bird to such an extent that when it was time for Mrs Duffield to move on, she begged her to leave the creature behind at Reginald Terrace.

And for Mam, that is the end of the story. In telling her tales she declines commentary, embroidery and spec-ulation. She sticks to the facts, and evokes such vivid scenes that listening to her, I am disinclined to speculate while she talks, lest I miss some wonderful detail. It is all better than any invented story, I believe, until I am drawn to the computer. Because I am by now a little better, less numb, Mam has made me laugh and forget myself. I am almost feeling ready to face the outside world. But I would rather approach it first, through the protective glow of the computer's soothing screen.

For no particular reason, I search for information about The HMS *Mauritania*, thinking it would be fun to supplement Mam's tale with pictures, with information, with *facts*. So what am I to do when I find that the boat was scrapped the year before Mam claims she stood on the deck, waving to the sea of hat-clad heads below? Do I take this fact to her and demand an explanation? After 75 years, should I tell her that her history is all wrong? Or do I accept her tales as a story and accept her story as part of my own, however inaccurate it may be? And if I accept that her story, together with its falsities and inaccuracies, that her story is also my story, will I shrink even further from myself or get closer to understanding this woman that formed me?

And as I speculate on what it means to not know one's own parent, one's own past. I realise something else. It wasn't the window cleaner at all. I'm suddenly convinced it was Mrs Duffield's own husband who swore at her through that bird. And it makes me sad to think, like me, in attempting her escape, Mrs Duffield carried the brute with her, albeit in feathered form. Just as my Mam's story is mine, and it is part of me, no matter whether I like it or not, no matter how true it is.

26.

Astaire

Little Yvette would sit on the stairs up to Dr Austerlitz's rooms while he made pickled herrings. She would know when they were on their way because The Doctor, who seemed ancient to little Yvette but was in fact merely middle-aged, would carry news-wrapped herrings, treacle, sultanas and vinegar up the steep staircase to his attic. Soon after, the pungent smell begun to drift lazily down the stairs. To reward her patience Dr Austerlitz would eventually emerge and give Little Yvette one of the cured herrings wrapped in grease-proof paper. These were a great treat.

Not that there was a lack of food at home. Unlike many of their neighbours, the family didn't struggle, because Big Yvette could nose out a bargain at 100 yards, and anything she couldn't buy, she grew. At Reginald Terrace the family enjoyed a table of a high standard: Big Yvette and Horace went to the market every Saturday and bought the best quality they could find. Their usual babysitter, Nancy, would watch Little Yvette and her brother until their parents returned, which was when Nancy would make her way home. Then one night, Horace and Big Yvette were late back from the market (perhaps waiting for closing-time bargains) and, because it was dark, Horace accompanied Nancy back to her house. Something ugly ensued—accusations were thrown by Nancy's father, perhaps implying Horace had taken advantage of the 16-year-old for which Nancy had to be punished. When the man took his belt off Horace would tell his family, he decided that it wasn't safe for the girl to be left alone with her dad. Which is how Nancy was granted a small space among the crowd at Reginald Terrace, as maid and au pair rolled into one.

Nancy was to be a God-send to Big Yvette because, when the fighting started, Horace with his RAF training was among the first to go. Eight-year-old Little Yvette was on holiday in Blackpool when war was declared and came home to a terrace house transformed. Little Yvette didn't know what 'war' was, but her Daddy had gone, and Mammy was smoking and crying. She'd never seen Mammy smoking before. In fact, she now realised, all the women were crying. Shortly after, Daddy came home on leave and shortly after that, his absence became routine. Visiting, he would leave his metal trunk in the hall. After a few visits, Little Yvette and her brother learned that if his hat was on top of his trunk, then they had to be quiet and not disturb their parents, because Mammy and Daddy had gone up to bed for a rest.

But even with a War in full swing, things weren't

too bad and besides, Little Yvette thrived on having her mother's full attention. At school she was having a few problems, although she didn't understand why. The problem was that she wasn't learning, the solution turned out to be a pair of glasses. These glasses liberated her from the blurred indistinct world she had been lost in, finally, she could see the blackboard and understand the tasks she was given to do.

She also begun to make friends, particularly with little girls whose daddies owned shops. Margaret Hicks' dad had the fruiterers, the Longbottoms ran the fish and ship shop opposite, and at the bottom of the road was Perks' butchers. Little Yvette's wise choice of friends meant that rationing didn't bite quite as badly at Reginald Terrace as it might have. Also, to make a bit of extra gravy for the table, Big Yvette had hens in the back garden who supplied rare and precious eggs for the house, but which were also sold to local householders for meat, as they were Bantam hens and very tasty.

And there were still entertainments and these were many. Big Yvette took Little Yvette with her to the Grand Theatre in Leeds to watch the variety shows. This was as well as going to the pictures three or more times a week. Sometimes they went to see the film, sometimes just to see the newsreels and catch up on what was happening with Daddy and the War, sometimes, if fuel was short, they went simply to keep warm. But even then the Irish coalman would give them a bit extra if Big

Yvette needed it. They were a fortunate household run by a woman whose toughness of spirit had been forged in rural Canada. A woman almost as old as the century and who had grown up knowing she could sew a dress from the sacking that Sears delivered the corn in. A woman who could scratch an existence from the very earth outside the backdoor if need be.

Even though she was as frightened as anyone, when the sirens sounded, Big Yvette would lead the two children and the tenants down into the cellar with their blankets and eiderdowns wrapped over Mrs Herman's hand-sewn nightdresses. During the bombings the depth of Mr Herman's fear hinted at shell shock. Big Yvette's fear was more practical—she realised that if the house was hit they would all most likely suffocate under the rubble. But they were told to hide in the cellar so that is what they did. At least Little Yvette and her brother enjoyed themselves: there were games to play and plenty of people to play them with because under the house, huddled in the dark, mothers and children, Jews and gentiles, men and women. All of them equal in their fear and vulnerability.

* * *

As the War dragged on, Little Yvette grew up. The fighting had just ended and her Daddy was on his way home— miraculously uninjured—when she enjoyed her first proper date. The way she tells it to me now, her friend Pauline left her no choice.

"I've arranged to meet these two blokes, and I've no one to go with. Will you come?" Pauline was older than Yvette and much more sophisticated.

"I have to take the bread in, I always take the bread in on Saturday, then I'll come,"not-so-Little Yvette demurely told Pauline. She took the bread in and before leaving wrote a note for her Mam. *"I've gone out with two men,"* it said, just enough to give Big Yvette a heart attack.

Yvette had changed into her favourite dress, which was white with a pattern around the hem of big blue ships, and the two set off to meet their dates.

The two chaps were in the Royal Navy, but before the war had worked for ICI and were clearly of officer class. They were strangers to Leeds and looking to be shown around by the girls. Pauline's man was fabulous looking, Cyril he was called, and he looked stunning in his naval whites. He was an elderly 32. Yvette's chap was plain but jolly and his name is lost to posterity.

The day started well when the men bought Pauline and Yvette a huge peach each from Leeds market before asking them, where would be good for lunch? Mam suggested a tea house where she knew they could get a meal for 2-and-thre'pence. Two old ladies played a piano and a cello to accompany the diners. It was the funniest thing the men had ever seen, and they ribbed Yvette mercilessly before taking the two girls to the Empire for the matinee variety show.

"Where can we go for tea?" asked Cyril after the entertainments.

"Don't you say a word," Pauline commanded Yvette under her breath.

"We could go to Polly's Bar..." Pauline casually suggested, and Yvette nearly choked at her cheek. Polly's was the most expensive place in Leeds, but off they went. The two officers, keen to show off, ordered lobster. Yvette managed to see the bill, and was shocked to see that the meal had cost 16 shillings: the equivalent of a week's rent for the Hermanns.

After tea, "Where shall we go now?" said Cyril, coaxing the girls into spending the evening with the pair. So the foursome went to the Mecca to dance to the live band and singers they had on a Saturday night. It turned out the plain date was a fabulous dancer. Pauline wanted to dance with him but Little Yvette, who was by then an accomplished ballroom dancer herself after years of lessons, hung on to him. She sailed around the floor with her Naval beau riding a wave of abandon in her dress painted with sailing ships. They danced one dance after another while Pauline stood smouldering with fury by the side of the floor, chatting to the beautiful, charming, two-left-footed Cyril. All too soon the two men had to leave. Before he got on his motorbike the plain one asked Yvette.

"Will you write to me?"

"Yes, I will," Yvette promised. And she did, for a while.

But the writing soon fizzled out, because Little Yvette was about to join the adult world and her expectations had already spoilt her for a plain boy, even if he could dance like Astaire.

27.

Money

Though my career at boarding school had started badly, in my absence, businesses of all kinds were booming. Home for the holidays, the impact of the ripples of the capitalist great leap forward of the 1980s had visibly impacted on my hometown. Inside Number 24 the browns and oranges of the 1970s were replaced with white walls, black furniture and a glass coffee table. The taste for clean stark lines reflected an air of optimism about what could be achieved with energy, vision and, of course, money. There was change in the air for our small family too. Andrew was already doing well in the army and had recently married a girl he had met while stationed in Scotland. He was still being posted all over the world: we got postcards from Kenya, Canada and Belize—places I would look up in the atlas, so I could picture him there, where ever 'there' was this month. Paul had moved in with his girlfriend Michelle and taken a job as a caretaker at a school. Mam's children mainly off her hands, she must have thought this was a good time to expand the business.

In this new north, the Tory government's drum of

financial opportunism and individual enterprise could be heard even as far out as the suburbs of Victoria Park Avenue. Rising levels of disposable income offered business opportunities to the hard working and ambitious, but *one* woman selling her body is limited by time and energy as to how much she can earn. In order to overcome this inconvenient law of economics, Mam was encouraged by a close friend to open a brothel. "But I've only got two thousand pounds," she complained. "Well, you can open a sauna then," was the no-nonsense reply.

With her two thousand quid Mam went into the sauna business alone after a financial partnership with a cross-dressing acquaintance fell apart. She had met this character when he offered to clean Number 24 for free. His work was free because he would swan around the house in sensible courts, a powder-blue Peter-Pan-collared blouse and a bubble-perm wig, decorously pushing the Hoover. His cleaning was thorough though, and we had all thought him harmless until Mam's money starting to go missing.

After she got rid of him, Mam was indeed alone in her enterprise. But eventually, she saw her hard work and industry pay off when she opened the door of 'Aristotle's' for business. A crown court judge was later to pompously intone: "I'm sure Aristotle would be spinning in his grave had he known his name was to become synonymous with a massage parlour." I give him more credit. I was seriously impressed with what she had achieved. I was also thrilled that the business was to be moved from Number 24 to proper professional premises: I looked forward to getting my home back, without the constant stream of punters, without constantly being sent to my room.

And actually, Mam wasn't new to running her own operation. In my lifetime she'd had a café, called The Wheel, and an ice-cream van with no name anyone can remember. Before me, she'd had a marriage bureau, as dating agencies were called in the sixties, and at one stage she'd owned several houses which were rented out to students. Also of course, the upper floors of 24 Victoria Park Avenue were let continuously to a travelling circus of lodgers. But Aristotle's was the first of her businesses I remember clearly. And its existence was, though not the first lie of my life, certainly the biggest.

Her business experience showed in her choice of premises. The shop was located in an area of semi-industrial units and offices on the edge of the city—within walking distance of major employers like Yorkshire Television, but not actually in the retail centre or a residential community. There was even a bit of glamour. In the offices a little way down the street was an advertising firm which had produced a series of iconic ads for Porsche and, as a result, there was a string of tulip-red Porsches parked along the road. Perfect then, for the purposes of selling sex: close to the market but not in anyone's backyard.

And along with working practices and the trade unions, sex itself was getting an overhaul. Down in London, uber-madam Cynthia Payne had turned the selling of sex into something that was more naughtily suburban than urban seedy. In her leafy Streatham street, an unlikely location for vice, Cynthia serviced a desire for sex and strong-discipline with humour and charm. She resembled no one so much as Margaret Thatcher with her sexy matron persona and freeze-dried hair. The collision of harlotry and industry was all around, and Mam, in her early fifties with an apprenticeship of cottage-industry prostitution behind her, was perfectly placed to exploit these trends.

Following Payne's example, Mam sought to make her establishment respectable. The location helped: next door there was, handily, a sandwich shop which also functioned as an outside caterer. Opposite was quite a smart pub, one of those new ones just starting to call themselves 'wine bars' which served pints of lager in glasses like big vases, instead of pints of bitter in glasses like Toby-jugs.

Above the front door Mam had invested in a smart, tan-coloured awning emblazoned with the name of the sauna in a classy, dark brown serif font. On the ground floor was a reception area furnished with a desk, telephone, appointment diary and chair. Behind reception, and hidden to the street, was a waiting room, a corner of which was partitioned into a small sun-bed cubicle. From this room were stairs which took clients up to the first floor. Here there were two 'treatment rooms', a hand-built Scandinavian pine sauna and a shower. It was all very tastefully done, all the rooms were white, with heavily gilt-framed prints on the walls. It was also spotlessly clean and very well organised.

28.

A Lesson Learned

I hoped my letter home about the bullying I was endur-
ing at school would make an impact. I was already old
enough to know that my accusations would have little
effect on the majority of the school staff. They, after
all, had stood around and watched what was happening without intervention. But I at least expected Mam to
take my side, and I was right. Mam sent the letter back
to school but addressed it to Mrs Black along with a note
in her own hand in which she made it clear she expected
the situation resolved. And I'll say this for her, when Mrs
Black swung into action, she didn't disappoint.

One typically chilly North Yorkshire morning all the
third-form boarding girls—which comprised me and my
seven dorm-mates—were told to go immediately to Mrs
Black's office. This was highly unusual, as Mrs Black
wasn't really the hands-on type. She rarely addressed us
directly, never mind intervened in matters of discipline.
As we filed into her office I knew what the talking-to was
going to be about, but the others looked nervous. We all
had our day uniforms on, so at least we looked the part

of good middle-class girls, but I knew a blast was coming and so I stood there and stared down at the threadbare rugs laying limply over the uneven flagstone floor.

Mrs Black didn't give quite the bollocking I expected. Some of her lecturing was about how sick and tired she was of hearing that pupils were 'unhappy.' "Happiness is not something you have a right to. It is something which passes for a moment in life and then, is gone," she said of all our hopes and dreams.

After implying that misery was our birthright, she tackled the subject at hand. "I couldn't believe what I have read, and I couldn't believe what other members of staff have told me has been said to Katy," she told my dorm mates, while I, grass, turncoat, scab, hung my head, staring into the black earth beneath the rugs. "I will not hear of these things being said to anyone, never mind a fellow pupil," she warned, and I believed her. If I couldn't trust Mrs Black to be on the side of right, who could I trust? She didn't let me down.

That day spelled the end of my racist bullying, but not, of course, of the everyday ups and downs of teen-age-hood, and there were still many ups and downs to fit in. But I learned an important lesson that day. I never forgot the staff members who had stood by while a twelve-year-old girl was routinely referred to as 'chi-chi' and 'half-breed'. I am describing here the house masters, matrons and teachers who looked calmly on while my torturers spent our nightly 90-minute prep looking through the big dictionaries, the old-fashioned kind which ran to several editions, searching for new words to attack me with. These grownups, adults who were entrusted with our care, were supposed to stand in place of our parents, only thought to mention what was going on *after* Mrs Black asked them about it. I got the message. There were adults who weren't sure if such behaviour was unacceptable, for some it may even have been a shock that this level of contempt for a darker skin wasn't merely horseplay, just part of the normal run of things. With such people around I couldn't expect protection. With their help, I learned never to take acceptance for granted. I left at the end of that term a bit wiser about my place in the world and with a lasting distrust for all manifestations of authority.

I had found out whose side I was on and so, when Mam showed me around Aristotle's, I was impressed with her little empire. It was obvious even to my teenage eye that she had worked her fingers to bloody stumps to fit out the building. All she needed now were to find the women who would bring the business to life. After the holidays, I returned to boarding school proud of her and with a new lie about how she afforded the fees, a lie I felt confident in. My Mam ran a 'health studio'. She was a business woman. There was no shame in that.

29.
Daily Life

I went back to school and Mam's step up in the sex industry settled into its stride. Aristotle's opened around 10am and closed some 12 hours later. On duty at all times were two women and a receptionist. The working women wore little white short-sleeved dresses, of the style that beauticians still wear, though these ones were shortened to well above the knee. My Mam stopped short at name badges. Emerging from the uniforms were hints of sensuality: seamed black nylons above teetering high heels, a peep of garter or soft pale flesh emerging from stocking tops. This uniform: a combination of Daz blue-white purity and tantalising glimpses of black and scarlet was a clever trick, hinting at forbidden fruit, while avoiding laying it out for the consumer too obviously.

Aristotle's taught me that selling sex is as sophisticated a process as selling any other product. Sex needs branding: Aristotle's, if not the Selfridges of the sex trade, could easily have claimed to be its John Lewis: honest value, reliably supplied. It had as little to do with the female bodies stacked high and sold cheap on the streets as the stall in Leeds market called '*Arrods*' had to do with the Mayfair store. So, sex is not simply sex, it has to be branded so that the consumer knows exactly what they are buying. Street trade was more visible then and Spencer Place, a few miles away in Chapeltown was the centre of Leeds' red-light district. Sex was more available there and cheaper, Aristotle's had to offer something more, and it did: privacy, cleanliness and safety from robbery and attack. It provided these things as much for the girls who worked there, as it did for the punters who soon began to seek the place out.

Mam soon found that the key to staffing Aristotle's was variety—for instance there was nearly always a dark-skinned black woman working there, but never I think an East Asian. (Though I remember a petite blonde woman who called herself Sian who believed she looked East Asian, when in reality her only allusion to East Asian ethnicity was that she looked little like Shirley MacLaine in *Gambit*. She lasted a while though so it seems the punters thought she looked East Asian enough. Perhaps she survived purely by virtue of making herself host of that particular fantasy.) Accordingly, there were fat women and thin women, big breasted and small, old and young—though this last was within reason. The lower age limit was early twenties and the upper, late forties. Each had their own rules about the services they offered and this was negotiated between them and their clients.

In the time-honoured tradition they split their earnings with Mam. Punters were also charged an entry fee.

These women, or 'the girls' as everyone connected with Aristotle's called them, spent the long hours sitting around talking, smoking and eating. As in every other area of life, food was important. Meals were much planned, discussed and anticipated as food was key to making a difference to the days. On Saturday nights, my Mam took in a Chinese takeaway for whoever was working and ate it with them. If I was at home, and never one to miss a meal, I would be there too.

Though they may have been busy in the evening and perhaps had a mini-rush at lunchtime, there were long days to fill when there were few customers. So the girls talked and talked. Not many of them worked more than a couple of days a week, and in their own time the majority were mothers and grandmothers, as well as wives and girlfriends, so there was plenty to talk about. One girl Ada, whose boyfriend was a writer whom she worked to keep, would bring his poetry in for us to read. I didn't think much of it, though the others thought it was great. I thought he might be better off, say, getting a job, but Ada seemed happy for him to stay at home, nurturing his talent. And who was I to disagree?

It is normal to cloak sex in intrigue and immorality—and no one, neither buyers nor sellers, wants sex to become as common as buying a loaf of bread. Intrigue increases interest and is almost as important as the act itself. As with any other saleable commodity, scarcity helps to maintain prices. However, it is difficult to describe just how normal everyday life at Aristotle's was. If you turned up with expectations of experiencing something dirty, something disallowed, the girls would be happy to accommodate. But if you arrived knowing that having someone listen to you is as important as, perhaps, a bit of hand relief for a happy finish to proceedings, then that was fine too. The fantasy which requires fulfilment is always in the imagination of the consumer. The supplier merely stands up from the low sofa, smooths her hands down her white overall, checks that there are no shards of spring roll stuck between her teeth, and climbs up the stairs to get on with the job.

30.

Older

The other half of my double life, boarding school, began to take on more colour as I got older. That was the way it worked, as we grew and worked our way through the school hierarchy, our horizons were allowed to expand a little. First, we were given responsibilities and allowed to boss junior pupils around. In the lower forms we were put into squads and each squad had domestic tasks to do. Each week, one squad was responsible for washing up after meals: a mammoth task, which was far worse before dishwashers were installed. There were other jobs too—ironing the boys' uniforms was one I particularly resented. They performed no personal tasks like this for us, so the sexist division of labour was built into the very structure of our day. The boys had different, more masculine, work. The worst was emptying the sump which collected grease and waste from the kitchen sinks. There was a pay-off waiting for us though. When we reached fifth form and crawled to the summit of achievement, we ran the squad.

As well as the extra responsibility, we were trusted

with more freedom, though the exact extent of our freedom was not written down and had to be tested through our actions. One thing that was tolerated, but not encouraged, was smoking. I took up smoking with the same enthusiasm some of the more popular girls reserved for hockey or riding. We had a tree that everybody smoked beneath—it was a monkey-puzzle tree, sky high with branches so dense that it offered protection from even the worst downpours. I have a line in my diary which still resonates—"Smoked five cigarettes yesterday. Think I'm hooked!" Twenty-odd years later and still struggling with my smoking habit, I cannot imagine why I reacted with such glee to becoming addicted to "smelling like a third-class railway carriage" as Mrs Black put it when she caught us one day while taking her pet Pekinese for a stroll. (Or rather, she took the Peke for a carry, since I never saw that dog walk. It lived either on a cushion beside her desk, or under Mrs Black's arm.) My need to achieve some form of status must have been very strong.

Academically bright students, a category of which I was proudly part, took 'O' level maths, French and Art early. Early being at the end of the fourth year, now known as Year 10, completing the rest of our O'levels at the end of fifth form. In between working for various exams, I managed to fall in love with a talented boy called Marcel, whose parents were French and obviously hippies, but who had unaccountably been brought up amongst the rainy clouds in the North of England.

Marcel obsessed me throughout fourth and fifth form. For those two years he was both the object of my affection and my nemesis. He was, I suppose, as much of an outsider as I, and with him I started a pattern that haunts my love affairs to this day. He had pronounced buck teeth and a slightly camp, theatrical way with him. Yearly we held a show in The Barn, the highlight of which was that one boy from each year was on that day, and only on that day, allowed into the girls' dorm to be made up and dressed as a girl. In the evening, the whole school gathered for a catwalk show where the boys would parade up and down the centre of the hall and the pupils would vote for the best 'girl' and in our year, it wasn't Marcel, but a talented cricketer who made the most excellent girl. In all things at school, aptitude at sport was the decider of who was a leader and who would be lead. The Miss Fyling Hall crown would therefore go to a sportsman, no matter who had the best legs.

Marcel first asked me out in the fourth year and we had a happy time together which comprised lots of snogging in darkened classrooms after prep. But we also shared a passion for art, and talking, and did lots of both together. Mainly though, we bonded over our rejection of the sporty culture of the school, revolving around rugby in the winter and cricket in the summer. In many ways we were lucky to have found each other.

It went wrong because, as always, I took him for granted, then I chucked him, fully expecting him to ask me out again. He did, but almost immediately, brutally, he chucked me. In a transparent move for revenge, he began going out with a very homely-looking girl from the fifth year, a year above me. This was a master stroke as hierarchy dictated that I couldn't take my anger out on her. So instead, I turned on him. I made every bit of contact we had fraught with tension. And the opportunities abounded: we had every class together, ate together as heads of the youngest pupils' dining table, and attended prep together every night.

What I could not, and still cannot, abide was his arrogance in assuming he could just take the decision to have nothing more to do with me, and I had to accept it. I have become slightly more mature now, and I know that without two people believing in it, a relationship simply ceases to exist, but I still cannot completely accept it. I thought then that I could bludgeon Marcel into submission with the strength of my personality. And of course, the more I attempted to bully him into submission, the faster he ran from me. And who could blame him?

All of this was played out in front of every other pupil. The littlest children in the school, who were aged between about seven and nine, were drawn into our conflict. They were children who hadn't yet formed the hard skin that boarding school demands.

Marcel and I ate breakfast and dinner with these

kids, our job was to help them butter their bread, and get the last scrapings out of their peanut butter jars, and in the mornings, read to them their letters from home. Some of their parents were clearly using the school as a kind of up-market social services, at least I can think of no other explanation for a father who sends his eight-year-old daughter secretary type-written letters which, due to the ridiculously formal nature of the language, the little girl has no hope of reading. Anyway, once hostilities began, Marcel and I would get the kids to race—girls against boys—up to the serving hatch for the food trays which Marcel or I would share out, depending on who won the race and got the food back to the table first. Some days the girls ate very well, with the poor boys left with the scraps. Other days, Marcel and the boys feasted like kings and the girls and I would still have rumbling tummies at bedtime.

Valentine's day came, and for the fortunate there would be a card about two-foot square and padded with cheap silky fabric waiting for them at breakfast. This would be opened in front of the whole school, so that the gaudy print could be admired by all. I was once fortunate enough to receive one of these cards: I can only see with hindsight that this card was a key to the acceptance I craved, as among the girls, popularity with the boys was all-important. I think I enjoyed the morning, but then the card itself made little impression on me and I quickly forgot about it. To Marcel, whose public declaration must have taken more guts than I possessed, my behaviour must have seemed more than dismissive. It was in fact cruel and I didn't deserve his adoration. For me, this was beside the point. I wanted him to want me, even if I didn't want him.

Through all of this, I managed to make a close friend of one of the school secretaries, Mrs Hodgeson. Dorothy was a Catholic, as I almost was, and as there weren't many at the school, she ended up being adopted by me. Dorothy would invite me and some of the other girls to her flat in Robin Hood's Bay, make us tea and give us biscuits, let us look through her jewellery box and try on her treasures. She was extremely kind to me, and became a key member of the alternative family I built for myself.

Other pillars of this family were Mr Hooley, our bearded headmaster. He was particularly kind to me on a couple of occasions when he need not have bothered, but he could be cruel when he needed a victim for one of his jokes. Crucially, I knew that he thought I was bright and could achieve. Others members of staff were not so encouraging. One self-important geography master, was taking a stroll around the class when he asked me what I wanted to do for a living. I was surprised, we were all heads down, getting on with a task. "A barrister," I said, though really this was what Mam wanted me to do. This snake took aim and with false encouragement dripping from his smiling voice said: "Well, if you aim for a thousand, a hundred will come that bit quicker," before moving away from me, crushing my dreams with every step.

I would regularly adopt adults, even before I went to the school. A lovely couple lived near us briefly in Leeds. That they were lesbians would have been news to me, I was too young to notice. I was just aware that these two women lived two doors away from us and would invite me into their house to play with stuff they'd collected, like the contents of their amazing button boxes. Also, like Dorothy, they fed me and so easily earned my devotion.

Still only in her early sixties, Dorothy died suddenly a matter of months after I left the school. Her loss was a blow but not a decisive one. I had picked myself up before and I would do so again. It is dangerous knowledge for a sixteen-year-old: To be aware that the loss of no single person is so appalling as to be terminal. That one can go on even when those closest are wrenched from us. But, not long before she passed, I had found a steely, ruthless place inside my heart where I could hide from feeling. I also knew that I might to need to shelter in this God-forsaken place again, so in a strange way I cherished it.

Because of boarding school, I experienced adults who, for want of nothing for themselves, took pleasure in the encouragement of others. From my fellow pupils I experienced the closest thing I had known to siblings of my own age. I also got to live vicariously through their stories of home. Not every girl in my dorm was from a perfectly functional family and there was little privacy, so, eventually we all heard about each other's problems. One friend would phone home on the once-a-week call; we had to walk over a mile to the phone box in the village to make each Saturday afternoon. Once we'd done the walk, we had to queue behind each other to use the single handset. (No wonder the villagers felt sorry for us—in winter this bedraggled ribbon of children must have been a pathetic sight. But of course, for the school it provided yet another non-activity to fill our time.) Phone calls were precious, and this girl would spend those few minutes of actual live contact with home trying to work out exactly how drunk her mother was.

Our problems were the kind you find everywhere. Another girl had found it so difficult to get on with her dad's new partner after her mother's death that she ended up boarding at the school just to get her out of this woman's way. She would cry intermittently for her mother, a quiet inconsolable whimpering which went on long into the night, breaking all of our hearts.

I could go on, but the point was that once I had understood the way that families sometimes failed to do the best for their most vulnerable members, I didn't feel so alone. I also gained a working knowledge of how groups were supposed to function, so that today, if I concentrate very, very hard, I can join in with a group with a degree of authenticity. During those years I did learn a more or less convincing way of being in the world, but I did not gain redemption. The truth now is the same as the truth then: I am an old soul and a repository of secrets.

31.

Ricky

When Little Yvette had stopped being little, but long before she was to become Mam, my mother met the first man she was to fall in love with. She was in her late teens; he was a decade older. He was well educated and spoke beautifully and being so, quite in line with her expectations. They met at a dance, as everyone did back then, and it was obvious to Mam he was a different class altogether than the honest working stock that had produced her. Brian had been to university and had a flat in Headingly, just behind the University.

Along with glamorous friends, Brian even had a car which came with his job as a journalist for the government-run Central Office of Information. He called Yvette 'My Little Brown Mouse' and had, early in their relationship, shaved his beard off to reveal a very handsome young man underneath the hair. My mother was lost in love.

But it was difficult for her to live up to Brian. One day he invited Yvette to drinks at the Metropole Hotel, which in the early fifties was the city's undisputed top destination for the best type of person. To make sure she at least looked like the consort of a man of Brian's stature, Yvette dressed herself up to the nines. She couldn't however do much about her youth, and Brian had worked in London, mixed with important people— he had *even* been abroad. At the hotel bar he introduced Yvette to a couple of smart-looking men, one of whom was the vice-consul of Greece. The other chap had brought his girlfriend, a sophisticated large-featured young woman who had just started a career as a movie starlet. My mother was in awe.

The topic of conversation turned to time that the friends had spent in London and Yvette kept quiet, hoping that looking the part and smiling would be enough. Eventually, the horsy young women turned to her and drawled:

"What do you think of London, Yvette?"

There was a pause, while the men turned to her and waited to find out if this young girl could talk as prettily as she sat.

"Very...er... big. And busy," Mam eventually stammered out.

Another pause as the three turned back to their conversation, which is just as well, as they would have seen her shrink back into her chair, and become Little Yvette again.

Brian had other advantages, though, even if Yvette couldn't quite crack his pretentious friends. At the beginning of every month he bought her a little present, then until his next pay-packet she would have to help him out. Mam was by now working as a typist in Leeds and living at home. Brian's money always ran out very quickly, in part because he had a serious drinking problem. He was fortunately the kind of drunk in whom inebriation is taken for personality, and certainly his almost continual drinking didn't seem to affect his work, as he was employed to use his RP accent on various local radio programmes.

And Yvette found that the likes of Brian could overcome a simple lack of money surprisingly easily. For instance, his local greengrocer would extend him endless credit, the balance of which he only vaguely kept track of. Perhaps equally enamoured by Brian's status, the greengrocer would overlook Brian's requirement to pay simply to keep him as a customer.

One night, the couple went to the Mecca where Yvette danced with a good-looking young man called Frederick Massey. The three, Ricky, Brian and Yvette got on well, although by this stage Brian and Yvette's year-long relationship was struggling under the weight of commitments unmade, words unsaid. Ricky told them he was a keen tennis player and Brian and Yvette went to see him play in a local tournament. He was a good player, but Brian could see more potential in this young man than his aptitude for sport. Ricky and Yvette got on like a house on fire.

"You should marry him, he'll be good for you," Brian told Yvette, under his breath. Yvette had until that moment rather hoped her husband would be Brian, but she could nevertheless see he had a point. Ricky was pleasant, handsome in a vital, Clark Gable sort of way, had a reliable income from his job as a maintenance engineer and, crucially, he actually wanted to be somebody's husband.

After that day Brian faded altogether from Yvette's life, but she intermittently kept up with his work and it seemed he never fulfilled his long-held ambition to work on the *Picture Post*. Yvette grew to hold for him a grudging gratitude that he had set her free. She recognised good advice when she heard it, and was as practical as her mother, so six weeks later she accepted Ricky's proposal.

32.
Nearly in the Picture

As I listen to her, I'm aware that my mother's story is almost catching up with me. Almost, but not quite. I grew up with Ricky, Mam's first husband, or rather, I grew up around talk of him, which is the same thing for a small girl whose internal geography is formed by the conversation around her. By the time Mam started telling me about her first marriage, I was already long certain this man was a martyr, if not a saint. Ricky was 'my Dad' to Andrew and Paul, but his absence also pressed in on me, their little brown sister. He had a presence on my landscape, this man I never met. A picture of his excitable brown eyes and dashing moustache has rested all of my life in the family photo album. When I was little, if the family faced a conundrum, then 'What would Ricky do?' was a reasonable way to frame the problem. I imagined him mulling the issue over, staring into the middle distance like Andrew does when he's thinking, absently playing with the corners of his 'tache.

Because I know what is coming next, my breath is bated, waiting for her to continue. I listen and love is washed up with memory. They are not my memories, true, but these are the stories which in my early childhood had only just left the present. This story, Ricky's story, carries a greater weight for me, it carries a greater weight for all of our little family.

The couple wedded in February 1952. Neither Ricky, who was only 22, nor Yvette, then just 20, wanted to wait. After all, in the six months since they had met, they had spent every single evening together. The service took place at The Holy Rosary church, Chapeltown. There were no long dresses: the men wore their best suits, the ladies their good frocks, best hats and a corsage. Yvette Turner and her single bridesmaid carried round posies of austerity flowers. After she became Yvette Massey, my mother's new status was celebrated by a sit-down meal for twenty at Polly's. The guests feasted on casseroled chicken, the only meat that the restaurant had to offer.

The newlyweds' three-day honeymoon was spent in London; the first time Yvette had visited the capital. On their second night, King George VI died and nearly every shop, theatre and restaurant in the capital closed as a mark of respect. Eventually, the young couple found a restaurant open in Chinatown and splashed out 32 shillings on a Chinese meal, a highlight of the trip.

Ricky and Yvette set up home together in a single room in Leeds before moving to their first proper house in Lower Wortley. Six, I am told, happy years later my brother Andrew was born and four years after this

Paul completed their family. Ricky was a keen amateur photographer so there are many photographs of my brothers as they grew up. You can flip through the album watching them transform from bandy-legged toddlers to boys on the cusp of young manhood. Andrew had dark brown hair and a pointed face, lit by a broad grin. As he grew his head, which in early childhood had been too big for his body, grew, or shrunk, into better proportion and his jaw became more pronounced, allowing his face to lose its pinched quality. Paul was blonder and rounder-faced than his brother, he smiles less and more often wears a thoughtful expression. In the pictures he never catches up to Andrew. He remains smaller, more questioning, his brighter moments never quite caught by the lens.

In the early sixties Ricky, Yvette and the boys moved to 24 Victoria Park Avenue and the house represented a step up in their status. Yvette always worked, so there were two wages coming in. The family settled into their new surroundings, while the boys thrived. Life was good.

33.

An Ending

I am continuing to listen to Mam with difficulty, for even while I anticipate my entrance into her tale, I know there must be another ending first. And there are events so shattering that, without a sensible ordering imposed in retrospect, they take on a kind of totemic quality, so that the lives of those affected are almost entirely defined by them. Time becomes bifurcated by such an episode, so that the difference between before and after comes to matter almost as much as the moment itself. So, on an afternoon in 1967, Yvette went to find Ricky in the garden of Number 24 where he was cutting-back some over-vigorous raspberry bushes. She wasn't to know that, simply by her passing on a telephone message, a defining sequence of events had already been set in motion.

I find it hard to sit still as Mam tells me how what happened, happened. I fidget not because I don't know what is coming, but because I do. And I know that bringing these things into sharp focus, rather than leaving them in the past, a past before I was even born, a past I should surely be allowed to ignore, will perhaps affect my view of her. I am used to thinking of Mam as terrifying, invincible. Now I have to face facts, it has become convenient for me to view her as a sort of monster. And I can continue to do so because I have never really listened to her properly before.

"Kenneth wants to know if he can come for a pint with you tonight?" Yvette shouted to Ricky.

"Tell him that's fine." Ricky was going for a drink with his sister's husband. Ricky's nephew Malcolm had already arranged to go with them. Kenny, Malcolm's brother was phoning because he wanted to join the gang on their night out. Yvette stayed at home with the boys. Soon, she put Andrew and Paul to bed as on any ordinary evening. But instead of going to bed herself, Yvette stayed up waiting for Ricky.

As the clock ticked around to eleven, she began to wonder where he was. It was already late for him, as Ricky didn't drink much because he couldn't really hold it and got drunk ridiculously quickly. By one in the morning she had begun to worry, but was relieved when there was a knock on the front door.

She went toward the porch and could see a policeman's helmet through the ribbed half-glass. He seemed to be leaning toward the glass, and Yvette assumed this was because he was supporting a drunken Ricky, who he'd perhaps picked up because he'd been wandering the streets of Leeds, lost. Thinking this, she opened the door easily, with no particular sense of dread. And standing before her were indeed two policemen, but they were alone.

"They were only young," she tells me now. "Kids really."

Mam showed the policemen into the living room, where one of them turned on the electric fire. He sat Yvette down in its meagre warmth before telling her what she had been waiting to hear since first seeing them on the doorstep.

"Your husband has been hurt in a fight. He died of his injuries."

And with a policeman's flat words my mother became a widow at the age of 35.

The shock made her involuntarily jump several inches into the air before landing back on the sofa. Her next thought was that she had to tell her six-year-old and ten year-old who were asleep upstairs. For a long time after that she didn't have any thoughts other than ones suffused with pain. A few weeks into her grieving, the process indelibly marked her body and her hair turned completely white. It remains so to this day, a trophy to the savagery of the cull of this young husband, this father.

Mam tells me he was a peaceful sort who had frequently told his boys that the really brave man is the one who walks away from a fight, not the one who stoops to violence. It was not surprising that the police took an interest in his death and it soon became clear that there were to be changes brought in the wake of Ricky's death.

It wasn't until the trial that the events of that night gained any focus. The four men had had an unremarkable evening, except for an argument between the two brothers, Kenneth and Malcolm. Kenneth had jeered at his brother that he was under his wife's thumb, that he was a door mat, a milksop. Ricky had left them to it until it was time to call it an evening and the quartet went out into the street in front of the pub. The brothers were still arguing, and Ricky mentioned to his brother-in-law that he was going to break it up by offering one of the brothers a lift. He never got the words out.

As he approached Kenneth, his nephew threw a punch which he claimed in court had been intended for his brother. Instead Ricky took the force of the blow. It broke his nose and caused him to fall back onto the pavement so hard that the back of his skull was shattered. He died instantly.

There were raised eyebrows at his account. Ricky was around 5'8" and Malcolm was over six foot, so it seemed unlikely that Kenneth could have mistaken one for the other. On the other hand, a drink had been taken by everyone and varying witness statements confused things. There was no thorough examination of the evidence in court as Kenneth pleaded guilty to manslaughter. He had served a short time on remand so he walked away from court a free man.

This was the family I was born into a mere three years later, into a place of recent mourning, of widow's weeds. A household of two fatherless boys and a woman still devastated by the loss of a man I never knew but whose name I carry.

34.

The Lift

It is a chilly Sunday afternoon in November and I am waiting outside Mam's flat for her to appear and to begin the long climb down the three steps outside her block and then the slow lowering of herself into the passenger seat of my old, none-too-clean Hyundai. I am giving Mam a lift to a church service she has decided she wants to attend. Or rather, re-attend. It will be thirty years since my mother last stepped foot inside a Kingdom Hall and she seems upbeat, jolly even, at the prospect.

Since she has been talking, I have come to see that under Mam's creaking gait and widow's hump, is the heart of a survivor as much as a warrior. I have thought her tough, mean even, though her meanness is a sin of omission. I realise that I have feared her not for what she did do but more for what she didn't do to protect my childhood from the harshness of the worldly seas on which our little family was buffeted about.

True, she provided no father for me other than one killed and martyred long since, no haven at Number 24, which I remember as even more of a brothel than

Aristotle's. There, sex was cellophane-wrapped and commoditised, not merely happening under my bedroom floor. Not that I was ever approached by Mam's clients, but nevertheless I felt an undertow of threat. That heavy wooden front door was the one I used, my hand turned the same handle they had pawed a moment before. After the day I floated out of myself and began to truly understand what my mother's business was, I always approached the front door with a slight sense of dread. I could never throw off the taint of that day, the breathing through the walls that continued long after the punter had paid his money and left.

So I know that the survivor in her has made her a fighter too, she is both perpetrator and victim. And she has cast me in her mould. So that today, on this harsh spring day, crisply cold and hesitant in its promise of summer, I know that under Mam's brittle smile she is not in the best of tempers. And under my pretence of helping her, neither am I. This trip out marks a milestone for us. I have been around for longer than my usual one-night visit and we really began to grate on each other days ago. But we haven't argued or rowed—a situation almost unique for us. I suspect my illness rendered me unsuitable quarry for Mam. I was unable to make the kill a sport and perhaps she wouldn't lower herself to hunting wounded prey. The service at the Kingdom Hall lasts nearly two hours and this seems to me to be two hours of freedom from her circling, her sniping, so I am happy enough to be a taxi. But my offer seems to have sparked something in Mam. She suspects perhaps that I am recovered sufficiently to re-engage with our usual hostilities.

While I wait in the car, drumming my fingers on the dusty dashboard, another vehicle parks behind me. I hardly notice it, as at almost the same moment I see Mam emerge from her front door. She is dressed in her Sunday finery: a short faux-fur jacket, scarf bundled around her neck and up to her face, almost up to her smear of bright red lipstick. Above her shocking-red lips, her best round gold-rimmed glasses sit perched on her prominent nose. Completing her ensemble are a calf-length velvet skirt, opaque black stockings and black court shoes slightly too long for her tiny feet, necessarily so, as her feet are almost as wide as they are long so her shoes have to be bought a little large to accommodate their girth. She is wrapped up to sit for hours in a freezing Kingdom Hall, but probably not warmly enough to endure the atmosphere inside the car. Under her not-too-carefully applied make-up, her face is thunderous. I realise I should have helped her out of the flat, rather than leaving her to it. She is not happy because I have been waiting rather than helping.

She opens the passenger door and, with much huffing and puffing, lowers herself slowly into her seat. I start the engine. We have not exchanged a word and every second that ticks by merely strengthens our resolve not to be the first to crack. I begin to turn the wheel in order to drive out of the space, but find that the car parked behind me has left me too little room to reverse. All I can do is repeatedly turn the wheel while moving a little way backward and forward until I can nudge the front end of the vehicle out of the space and into the road. On the second attempt I begin to swear quietly under my breath. On the third attempt, I turn and turn the steering wheel, and make myself a silent promise that my next car will have power steering. Now my mother begins panting heavily, her breath coming in long loud wheezes, while she clutches her handbag to her chest with one hand and the other rests on the door handle, as if ready to leap for freedom at any moment.

"What's wrong?"

I am terse but under my sceptical tone I am more than a little worried that she might be having some kind of 'turn'.

"Nothing!" She shouts while staring wild-eyed out of the car windscreen, panting and gripping the door handle so hard, her knuckles turn white.

I try a calm explanation:

"I'm just trying to get out of this space. The car behind has...."

"I'm fine," she bellows, and her face promptly turns bright pink.

I misjudge the next turn of the wheel and hit the kerb. I begin to swear. Mam suddenly finds the breath to resume attack and starts shouting at me.

"Oh Kate, you're such an aggressive driver. And I'm not the only one who thinks so." As she says this she shakes her head sadly, but before I can answer her, she resumes her wheezing breath performance all over again. I realise that she is trying to register 'fear' with this act, but it just makes me even more irritated. We are stuck between two parked cars on a suburban side road. It is probably the safest place we could probably be.

"Mam, would you get out of the car please while I do this manoeuvre?"

The request comes out in a menacing tone because my jaw is clenched painfully tight, so she leaps out of the vehicle at several times the speed she got in. In the ensuing calm I manage to free the car with one turn. Just beyond the space I stop and turn to look out of the passenger window, expecting Mam to be waiting on the pavement. She isn't there. I quickly look all around but she is gone. Fighting the urge to simply drive around the block and park the car again, I get out and see Mam at the top of the street. I shout to her, causing passing Roundhay residents to tut-tut disapprovingly at me. Mam looks around too, sees me, then turns and carries on walking up the street, toward the bus stop. She does this even though it's Sunday, and there are few buses anyway, and none at all that go in the direction of the Kingdom Hall.

A single, thoughtless second and I am running up the street after her, as indeed she intends. Hare-and-tortoise style, she can move deceptively quickly when she wants to and she crosses the street ahead of me. It takes another couple of minutes of my half-jogging behind her until I am close enough to talk.

"What are you doing?" I splutter between wheezes.

"You told me to get out of the car!" She yells, no longer breathless, just determined.

"Until I'd got the car out!" my voice has risen almost to a shout. More passing pedestrians stop to stare at me, a grown woman shouting down at a little old lady, a muffled septuagenarian, who appears to have been putting on layers of clothes for years.

When she is sure I am thoroughly rattled, have been shown up and stared at, Mam turns away from me and walks calmly back towards the car. She takes her seat with the graceful ease of a prima ballerina, leans back into her seat and, eyes closed, smiles serenely. Her need to clutch at the door handle and her handbag like twin airbags has also gone. It is as if my angry explosion has released her from her fury.

Too much of the time I spend with my mother is spent like this. I never know what reaction is required before she will cooperate—do I need to shout, burst into tears or walk away? It is a lottery, but once she's got the response she needs, an eerie self-satisfied calm inevitably descends. We pull away finally and I slump over the wheel as I drive, exhausted. And, as usual, Mam eventually begins chatting as if nothing has happened—she's looking forward to the service, what shall we have for tea when she gets back? I tune out and offer up a non-believer's prayer that we will complete the journey without incident.

"...And a lady came to the house last week who has been out of the church longer than I have...." This piques my interest and begin to listen to Mam's prattle. I am aware that two Jehovah's Witnesses have been visiting her on a weekly basis, tempting her back into the fold.

35.
G. O. D.

When I was very little, God had a central role in our family. The household I grew up in was chaotic, but also observant. Then came Mam's career change from secretarial work to prostitution, and my brothers leaving home and making their own lives, and finally, I left for boarding school. Then, all of a sudden, no one was around who cared about observance, or discipline, or the Bible, so at 15 years old I took it upon myself to get baptised.

This didn't surprise anyone. We had all—Mam, Andrew and Paul—found a spiritual path of some kind or another. For Mam it was to be another thing she neglected but eventually came back to, for Andrew it was a moral education he received young and which he still carries with him, and for Paul, well Paul is the one I know for certain believed. His belief in an afterlife, a paradise where loved ones are reunited and there is no pain, this faith was absolute and perhaps, in the end, deadly.

Mam joined the Jehovah's Witnesses in the mid-sixties when she was a young mother at home with Paul. He was in the pram in the back garden when a young woman called at the door. "Would you like to live in an everlasting paradise?" she asked. Mam thought she did, and she and her first husband Ricky signed up.

Ricky lost interest while Mam carried on going. He hated her adherence, on one occasion beat her black and blue for the sake of it, and this only concretised her belief. The more non-believers carp, the more the righteous are confirmed in the true path to glory. After all, being saved by Jehovah and enjoying the fruits of heaven can't be easy can it? Otherwise everyone and anyone would want a piece. By the time I came into this odd little family, Mam and the boys were established as devout Witnesses.

And being a Witness was hard work. For instance, we didn't celebrate Christmas until I was eight or nine years old and Mam had fallen out with her brethren. As a little child, perhaps eighteen months old, I remember spending a lot of time underneath the coffee table while my Mam talked about God with other witnesses who visited the house. As I got a bit older, we were at meetings twice in the week: Bible study on Tuesday and ministry training on a Thursday. On top of this were long meetings on a Sunday of at least a couple of hours, then there were doors to knock on and non-believers to convert. I don't remember very much of these doorstep encounters, just the frequent click of Yale locks as yet another door politely closed in our faces (few were slammed, most were never opened) and the gaudy illustrations on the cover of *The Watchtower*, which it was my job to hold up as Mam asked the householder: "Would you like to live in an everlasting paradise?" One *Watchtower* cover in particular fascinated me: It depicted those who would be resurrected after the end of the world, which, of course, was forever imminent. The picture showed corpses coming to life and emerging zombie-like from their graves, pushing aside slabs of marble bearing their names and clambering out so that they could take their rightful place in the Kingdom of Heaven, which was represented as a maddeningly indistinct bit of cloud on the horizon.

And then of course I have God to blame for Mam and my father Cyril meeting. If it seems unlikely that two people as different as my Mam and Cyril Anglin met and somehow produced me, then you-know-who is the common link: both were Witnesses and had corresponded as pen pals until meeting at some kind of rally or conference for adherents in London. At this single meeting, when my brothers were around the ages of eight and twelve and my Mam had been a member of the faithful for some time, they somehow conspired to produce me. The situation was less than perfect: Cyril had a wife in Jamaica with whom he had two boys much older than me, and Mam lived in Leeds with her two white boys. The prognosis was not good from the start, even I can see that.

Though his wife stayed on the island, he lived in London and I think they may have eventually divorced, at least that is what my father made known. On hearing of my imminence, he had wanted to be with my mother, or so he said, but she kept me and jettisoned him. So I never saw my mother and father together, and even now, to bring them together in the same thought is wrong somehow, like mixing tartan with stripes. They are both from completely different areas of my psyche. One is the known universe, that of Mam and my brothers, and everything else in this book. The other is my Dad's world, which can never be known but which is conjured in my imagination and dreamt of and wondered about and so will never lose its interest.

Despite the strictures of being a Witness, I was surprised to hear that, when the congregation my mother belonged to discovered my mother's condition—she was a single mother of two white boys having a black baby—they enthusiastically rallied round. One family gave her a Silver Cross pram they longer needed, another gave her lifts to and from the Kingdom Hall while pregnant (carrying her while she carried me). Three couples even offered to adopt me, sight unseen. After I was born and introduced to the congregation they passed Daddy's Khaki Princess from one to another as women do, enchanted with the little picaninny who ate whenever she got the chance and rarely cried. If they noticed my Daddy's absence, it went unremarked.

Despite all of this study and worship, I was sent, paradoxically, to Catholic comprehensive schools, as my mother had been. Neither of us was to make a good Catholic, but even I could tell that Catholicism, in comparison with being a Witness, was an easy ride. The services were more entertaining; the smell of incense, the priest's graceful robes, the pretty altar boys decked out like the miniature priests everyone hoped they'd become. And the glorious statues! In one corner a white, hippie-looking Christ stands wearing a crown made of thorns, crying blood and pointing to the sacred heart exposed at his chest, in the other corner a beatific Virgin bears down, tall and slim and dressed like a nun in blue.

The modern, unornamented interior of the Kingdom Hall couldn't compete with flickering candles and a soaring organ. At the Hall, you were lucky if there was a single vase of flowers on the plain table which stood in front of row upon row of utilitarian plastic chairs. At the Catholic mass, a gaggle of Irish ladies competed to produce the most abundant arrangements, so that carnations and lilies dripped onto every surface. These same ladies cleaned the church, replenished the candle supply, laundered the priest's robes and attended mass daily. They were always sat in the front two pews, black lace veils covering grey heads bent in supplication. Because of these ladies and others like them, the Catholic church of my childhood felt constantly alive with a kind of fervour. Even empty, the beauty of the churches contributed to achieving a Godlier state.

In Catholic school I was something of a rarity, a

non-Catholic and a Jehovah's Witness. Typically, I enjoyed my status as the wayward sheep which had yet to join the flock. The nuns who occasionally taught us felt it their duty to save my soul—just like the tallies of African souls the missionaries wrote to us about saving. They actively pitied me because I, a poor innocent lamb, was being brain-washed by 'the Jehovahs.'

But it wasn't until I got to boarding school that being a religious outsider became truly satisfying. As an almost-Catholic, I didn't go the church in Robin Hood's Bay that the other two-hundred or so Church of England pupils attended. Instead, the ten or so of us Catholics got in a mini-bus and were driven half a dozen miles or so to the church in Whitby which was presided over by the comically-named Canon Lovelady. The minibus was a big deal, we didn't have to walk up and down the peril-ously steep hill between the school and the Bay like the Church of England pupils. We had the same bus driver over the four years I was there. He never talked to us, and always played the same tape: a country and western compilation.

"You gotta know when to hold 'em/Know when to fold 'em/Know when to walk away/Know when to run/ You never count your money/When your sittin' at the taa-a-ble/There's time enough for counting when the dee-eal-ing is done," we sang along happily with Kenny Rogers and memorised his guide to a life as a successful card-sharp. Or: "Joleen, Joleen, Joleen, Jooo-leeeeen!

I'm beggin' of you please don't take my man." This was my favourite. The crescendo of pain Dolly Parton unleashes as she begs her more beautiful rival to leave her man alone still touches me.

To this day, I know 'D.I.V.O.R.C.E', 'Love is like a Butterfly', 'Jolene' and 'The Gambler' off by heart. None of the songs were exactly in line with church's teaching of course, but the music of our drive was ultimately accepted. I think the congregation in Whitby was happy to see us: back then, there were few young people among their number, and I think perhaps we helped to stave off an atmosphere of merely waiting for God. More likely they pitied us poor motherless wretches, turning up during term time in our scruffy blazers and stained ties, our noses reddened by the freezing temperature in the minibus and then snottily thawed out courtesy of the church's central heating.

Our priest Canon Lovelady, would weekly read out a list of parishioners who were ill and in need of our prayers. I prayed fervently, and as the time approached for me to leave boarding school, and the happy camaraderie of the minibus and the old ladies who fussed over us, I decided that I wanted to be baptised. There was no moment of transcendence, no epiphany. It was the simple fact that people were now accepting of me. That was enough. I had existed with lies and secrets for quite a while by the time I was fifteen, so it wasn't a huge stretch to believe in the unseen. Also, I was good at dogma: I could remember my Catechism and easily repeat word for word the questions and answers we learned by heart at Sunday school.

"What is a sacrament?'

"A-sacrament-is-an-outward-sign-of-inward-grace-ordained-by-Jesus-Christ–by-which-grace-is-given-to-our-soul,"I chanted.

Unlike the Witnesses, who seemed endlessly to study the Bible and debate its literal meaning, being a Catholic didn't require me to think. I could just relax into it and enjoy the certainty of the teachings and the music (little snob that I was, I particularly enjoyed singing The Gloria in Latin). Being a Catholic required that I simply accept God, rather than struggle to attain some impossible level of goodness, of holiness. Finally, after Mass, Sunday school offered the opportunity to drink orange squash, eat biscuits, steal altar wine, and shine intellectually. I was a fan of my new religion.

Given the circumstances of my conversion, it's not surprising that my Catholic fervour lasted no longer than my time away at school. Immediately after I left, there was no more appeal. On the one occasion I did go to Mass at home, I found there was no sense of theatre, standing alone at the back of a near-empty urban church. Being ignored was no fun.

Also, during my last term at school there was an embarrassing incident with Canon Lovelady. One of the aspects of Catholicism I had taken to with fervour was confession. In confession, not only did you get to talk about yourself a lot, but after saying a few Hail Marys and Our Fathers your sins were wiped clean. A fresh start, a new one every week if you fancied it.

On this occasion I had confessed my usual list of sins: taking the Lord's name in vain, being mean to another girl in my dorm, not respecting my teachers enough, that sort of thing. I stopped talking and waited for the usual admonishment to behave better, to say a couple of Hail Marys and Our Fathers, after which I would be off, with that brand new, gloriously cleansed feeling I loved so much. Instead Canon Lovelady let leash a mini-sermon on resisting the evils of the flesh. I had only kissed two boys and there had been nothing in those kisses which required resistance, yet his tone suggested that I was currently navigating a treacherous path which could easily lead to damnation. Or perhaps, when Mam came to my baptism he had seen something in the way her hip-swayed when she walked, or her too-red lipstick, indicating defiance rather than penitence that he wanted to warn me against. Mam fitted in well among the statues of Christ's bleeding heart, the red of his chest and the lipstick matched but she clashed horribly with the Virgin Mary, who's blue habit and eyes cast down in modesty and suffering were the total opposite of Mam and everything she stood for.

In any case, all the Cannon succeeded in doing was scaring me off. This was a modern church, so there was no modesty screen or grille to protect the penitent. It was one thing to be punished for sins one had actually committed (or omitted, depending on the nature of the transgression). It was quite another to have to listen to my priest talk about sex while I knelt burning with embarrassment just a couple of feet away from him.

I suspect also that it was being an outsider in the church that gave it its appeal. Once in, there was no more will-she-won't-she intrigue. I was simply expected to toe the line and be a good Catholic along with everyone else and I was never good at doing what I was told.

36.
The Bill

While I underwent a religious conversion, my mother's business was thriving. And Aristotle's quickly became the centre of my world when I wasn't at school. My mother's daughter, I couldn't let a financial opportunity go, so when Mam offered to pay me £5 a time to act as receptionist on a strictly casual basis I jumped at the chance. This role required little of me: I would tell the punters who was working that day, as most had their favourites, take their money as they came in through the door and direct them upstairs. The rest of the time I would sit and talk to the girls. It was a free education.

Pamela talked for hours about other places she had worked, previous jobs she had, and about her wonderfully camp little boy Richard, who I babysat from time to time. Rose told me about working in London and Glasgow from a shared flat with other girls or on the streets—far from judging neighbours and her huge Catholic family. I was sometimes goggle-eyed at their tales but I at least had the sense to shut up and listen, especially when the conversations took a more surreal turn.

"You know him has the newsagents at the back of Morrisons?"

"I don't know him. Go on though."

"You do! Big fat man. Swaps the dodgy videos."

"I don't. Go on!"

"You do. Well, you know he's selling school girl's knickers for four pounds a pair?"

"Why? Can't you just buy them in a shop?"

"No, these are worn. 'Soiled' he calls it in the ad."

"No!"

"Well I went into the shop the other day and nobody's behind the counter. I wandered up to the stockroom door, and there he his, hunched in the corner like Rumplestiltskin rubbing gorgonzola cheese into the gusset of some pound-shop pants."

"God! What did you do?"

"I asked him what he was doing. He knows I do this so I suppose he isn't bothered. So he says, 'I'm rubbing cheese into these knickers.' Then he stops, looks up at me and says: 'You won't tell anyone though, will you?'"

We had a good laugh, but really it was characters like this who peopled our day. There are so many men and women on the fringes of the sex industry, keeping their heads down, breaking bread with their families, buying *The Daily Mail*, playing the moral guardian. There are the strictly legit types: the accountants, landlords and suppliers that come with any business (stocks of baby oil, talcum powder and condoms need to be maintained). And there were people, mostly men, who just liked hanging around. Men like Harry The Spiv, who sold ludicrously overpriced 'contact' mags full of ads for gorgeous nymphomaniacs seeking adult fun. The adverts were entirely fictional. Nevertheless, his box numbers received plenty of mail, all containing hopeful, if misguided, stamped addressed envelopes. This meant that Harry, to avoid arrest or just a good beating, had to reply to at least some. He wrote many himself, but the risk of sending several similar letters in an identical handwriting to the same punter was ever present. His solution was to take writing pads, pens and the SAEs down to his local pub and get the middle-aged alkies that propped up the bar to write the letters he needed in exchange for free drinks. More than once, he gave me a bundle to post on the way back to school so that the postmarks would show they had come from across the North, and not solely from East Leeds.

We were a proper community at Aristotle's and my mother was matriarch. Thanks in large part to her judgement, there were no fights and almost no thieving. I am willing to bet that the incidents of STIs, mental illness and addiction at the sauna were less than on the streets outside the door. Most importantly, the sauna and the experience of that community normalised the sex industry for me. Actually, me and the girls normalised the sex industry for each other. Stigma meant that we had many conversations that we could only have in that back room, with other people who understood the business. I believe I saw Aristotle's for what it was: a place where good looking, decent women who could hold a conversation offered various sexual services in exchange for money. They could work hours that fitted around child care and earn enough to live well above the breadline. For the punters, Aristotle's was something forbidden, a trip to the edge of criminality and deceit, a sophisticated artifice, and perhaps the best brothel in Leeds for a while. As for myself, I experienced nothing which jarred with my religious convictions.

But it was hard work. Mam got up several times in the night to run hundreds of towels through the washing machine at home. She went to wholesalers to buy industrial-sized bottles of bleach and tile cleaner. She continuously hired and, on occasion, had to fire a stream of women who all thought that working in a sauna was easy money, many of whom quickly discovered it wasn't. She booked adverts in the local paper, she kept accounts, the whole lot. Mam was as far I was concerned a brilliant business woman right up until the day Aristotle's was raided by the Vice Squad.

From the beginning, the place made money—but not much. Despite my hopes that I would get Number 24 back, Mam stayed in business for herself at home. She had to. From the sauna she made about £120 pounds a week plus the payments on her new car. That wouldn't have kept me in school fees. She invested quite a bit in the decorations though, on the way up to the first floor treatment rooms the hall was filled with over-painted Victorian prints in heavy gold frames.

"Does your boss collect art?" one of the punters asked Rose.

"Oh yes. She only sends the ones she doesn't want here," she told him, never missing an opportunity to do public relations for Aristotle's.

But all the PR in the world wasn't going to spin the police, they had their sights on the sauna from the day Mam set up shop and on the day Aristotle's was raided it made the front page of the *Yorkshire Evening Post*. Ten policemen burst in simultaneously through the front door and an unused back door upstairs. An elderly doctor, a regular of Pamela's, got the shock of his life. He was allowed to dress and leave after giving his personal details. Instilling worry into punters is always a goal of police raids—after the publicity of such raids, they know the regular punters who are the bread and butter of a business like Aristotle's will be too scared to come near the place.

The police took Mam to the police station and presented her with their notes. They'd got their evidence in advance by sending two of their over-worked constables into the sauna to pose as punters.

"I'm sick of only getting handjobs—that's all they'll pay for," one officer of the law complained of his employers. Understandably, Mam had little sympathy. They already had days, times, sums of money that had changed hands, but this didn't stop them questioning Mam for hours and dragging up everything they could, including the death of her first husband, and a minute enquiry as to exactly why Pamela was wearing stockings at the time of the raid.

The worse part for her was when they put her in the cell. "Get in there," said one of the officers. "I haven't killed my brother you know", said Mam but he ignored her and pulled the cell door shut. They had put her in one of the men's cells with an awful wooden bed. She had had enough.

"What's she doing now?" she heard someone's voice enquire.

"Crying her eyes out," came the anonymous reply. And it was true.

It might have been the questioner who came and moved to her a women's cell. A stainless steel toilet and a woolly waffle blanket lent it an air of relative luxury. He brought her food too. Bread with Stork margarine on it and salad so bland it was like water on the plate. She just had time to reflect that the salad could have been improved no end by a spring onion or two, when one of the kinder officers came to tell her she was free to go. "We don't usually get people like you in here," said the young man who escorted her to the Desk Sergeant.

And that was the problem with the whole business really, as Mam says now: "We weren't the types to go to prison," so a career as a criminal Queen Pin was never really on the cards. She opened up the next day, of course. But a fine of £2,000 and being raided for a second time would eventually shut Aristotle's down for good and force the good women who worked there in safety into other, less reputable establishments, or out onto the streets.

37.

Somewhere to Run To

I am still at Mam's. I had returned to my own home but somehow came back to Leeds and Mam's little flat more and more often, looking for something I knew I was unlikely to find. The flow of her storytelling has stalled somewhat now that I am in the picture. Her memories of my father seem to be even more indistinct than mine. Mam tells me I look like him, but how would I know? He was much, much older than her. I don't know exactly how much older, but it is likely he was well into his fifties when I was born, compared to my mother's tender 37. I am not surprised she expected she could do better, even with the multicoloured family she had in tow. Remember, she was devout. She believed that Jehovah would provide.

So I have a gap where a Dad should be—but that at least gave me something in common with my brothers, who, once I arrived, seemed to adore me. When I was very little we spent a lot of time together, as Mam worked full time as a secretary before her change of career, so my brothers often baby sat. They demonstrated their adoration by buying me sweets from Binns' news-agents. This was a good thing. And they adored me by putting me in Mam's wardrobe, but not locking it. For if it were locked, I wouldn't have been able to open the door, which in turn would mean Paul had no excuse to shoot matchsticks at me from a 'gun' made of clothes pegs and elastic bands. He did this whenever I tried to leave the wardrobe and the game could go on well past the point of boredom, at least on my part. They also shut me in the blanket box, shooting matchsticks at me when I dared to lift the lid. Then they gave me home-brewed wine and got me drunk before I knew what 'drunk' was. I was apparently hilarious before being copiously sick and being put to bed by Mam, at an age when going to bed was the worst thing that could happen to me.

The Andrew and Paul I remember are far from ordinary. Each has their idiosyncrasies: Paul's apartness, his obvious isolation, a separateness that seethed from every pore of his flesh and invisibly covered his body like a shroud, so much so, that we didn't really notice it—it was just Paul. And Andrew's enthusiasm and bravery: there was nothing Andrew wouldn't try, taking apart a car engine, building a wall, especially when he had no idea how to and no experience either, so, when he joined the army and started jumping out of aeroplanes and fighting wars for a living, his choice didn't seem odd. And while I bonded with this pair of boisterous teenage boys, I barely noticed that in other people's houses there was a man in charge, a bloke, and not only that, one who ran things. This seemed amazing to me. I remember going to tea at a friend's home while I was at primary school. At her house, not only was tea eaten at a table, but the table was laid according to a strict family hierarchy. Dad sat at the head and had a bigger chair than everyone else. The chair had arms and he sat back in it, lounging over one of the arms as if on a throne. All he was missing was a lop-sided crown. 'Mum' sat next to him, all the better to bask in his reflected glory, and us children were arranged around him like visitors at his court.

Food was dished up according to this pattern as well: I simply couldn't believe I was expected to eat what was put in front of me when nobody had even asked me if I liked it. (Though of course, I did like it. I was a glutton after all.) Worse, what was put in front of me was about a third of the amount the adults had on their plates. I gobbled the paltry portion while greedily eyeing the adults' plates and ruminating on the unfairness of my friend's home life. The very, very worst thing, even worse than the small portions, was that only the Father spoke through meal time, droning on dully about something boring, like the news. So this was what you got if you had a Daddy who wouldn't let you watch telly at mealtimes. My Daddy, as you know, was dead not long after this. I shed a few, a very few, tears when Mam told me he was gone, but I am ashamed to reflect that I didn't feel his loss as keenly as I felt that tiny portion of dinner.

But, now I am supposed to be a grown up, I am aware of his absence again—a father who could sit at the head of the table, a man who can be trusted. And now I am in the picture, Mam's version and my version keep colliding. We build up to the sensitive stuff slowly, but still butt horns. "Was my Dad very short?" I ask.

"Oh yes, only five foot four."

"And he was kind when you met him?"

"It depends what you mean by kind. But when he didn't pay your maintenance, Andrew said, 'Never mind Mam. We'll manage. And we've got Katy. He's missing out.'"

So back and forth me and Mam went, with eager questions, gnomic replies, surprising and unasked for gems of information. But this is not enough for me. I am sure there is a way I can feel closer to my Daddy. I am sure there is at least one place I haven't tried.

38.
Exile

It was true that it was time to leave this country. The last straw came when I was in a shop, an ordinary fags and booze type place, queuing to pay for something. There was a young man behind me, late teens or early twenties, clad in sportswear, baseball cap jammed onto his head. He seemed to be in a rush, jangled his keys, hopped from one foot to another. I would have had no reason to notice him, had he not said what he did.

"Can you smell something?"

He addressed the middle-aged woman serving me. Until her face turned red and she slid her eyes down from me to the counter, I had no idea he referred to me.

'There's a right stink in here," he reiterated.

Cowed by embarrassment, the shop woman handed me my change. She seemed to grow smaller as the rage filled my chest. I felt my ears turn pink, as I calmly took my money, thanked her and exited the shop, taking my stench with me.

If, as you read this account, you wonder what the etiquette is for encountering racist abuse, it is this:

endure. Those around you, while they may not approve, will be stifled by reserve into silence. If you do not do the same, you will mark yourself out as doubly different, not just brown but also chippy. If you argue, if you complain, you may start to be regarded as a bit lippy, maybe even deserving of being taken down a peg or two. One who doesn't mind drawing attention to themselves and perhaps needs to learn that they are tolerated as guests. As such, it is bad manners to point out the frayed counterpane, the dodgy lampshade, the single bad apple spoiling the crate. So you see, you must endure, for if you do not you become deserving of disdain.

On such occasions—and they are not many, just often enough to remind me that I would sometimes rather be anywhere else but here—I doubt my patriotism. Don't get me wrong, I do love this country, but I think it is with a kind of expediency. I have affection for the scruffy urban glamour of Leeds and the rural ways I learnt in North Yorkshire and everything in between. I love the language it has given me, the humour every ordinary person shares—especially in a disaster, when we talk to one another without suspicion. I have lived the length of this island and I love the winter sunshine of freezing Yorkshire winters, when the mist sits, bad-tempered and unmovable across the dales. I love the summers in Brighton, when it feels like the whole world has come out to play and everyone smiles. Big, unwieldy families from Southall and Lambeth, posher people dressed up for the weekend down from the home counties, lovelorn teenage couples and gangs of twenty-something singletons. Folk who have come to shop, have a game of footy on Hove Lawns, spend money on tooth-shattering rock, smoke spliff on the beach or watch the beautiful carcass of the West Pier fall gracefully into the sea. But this love of country is heavily negotiated: it has to work around that boy in the shop and others like him.

Certainly sometimes, I do not feel I belong. What I know about fitting in, about how to be British, has had to be learned. I have also more than once endured the punishment of not belonging—of saying the wrong thing, or laughing too loudly, of not queuing properly. Then I am reminded that though I think of this as my country, there are those who do not agree. That to look different is to somehow be cast outside of normality, so that one can be totally relaxed at, say a dinner with friends, when another guest will make a thoughtless remark about 'ethnics' or 'asylum seekers' or 'immigrants' or whatever group they deem worthy of subjugation that day. (And the words do change, when I was a child I was half-caste, sometimes a picaninny, now I am as likely to be taken for straight-forward black, 'Arab' or, of course, a 'Muslim'.) The effect is sudden and inevitable, like rapid freezing, when moments before one had been calmly sailing a boat with ease. Such a comment can have me glancing around the room, in the hope that another pair of dark, recognising eyes will fall on mine in sympathetic acknowledgement of the fact that when they talk of gypsies, Jews, foreigners and others who don't belong here, they are talking about my mother, my father, me.

But worse, though I love this language I have inherited, and have no other language, I am aware that it is missing something fundamental. I am trying to write about myself and this language fails me, I can't even describe something so mundane as how I look. My skin isn't white—if you take this to mean all the shades of flesh between putty and dark apricot. Even if you include the dark-haired-dark-eyed-olive-skin combination of the Mediterranean, that still does not describe me—I am not 'swarthy' as my Granny Yvette used to say. And I am not black either—if by black you mean those skin tones between milk chocolate and blue-black aubergine, stopping at molasses on the way. These are decorator's words, but they'll have to do. They are all I have.

I can't see myself from the outside, so I don't really know how others see me. But I am bound to try and imagine what they see. When the thoughtless dining companion replies to my gentle remonstration (and I will be gentle, humorous even. I am aware I have to keep on the right side of those who may say: 'Look at the chip on her shoulder') in an effort to include me, that person I have forced to see my difference may grudgingly reply: 'I don't mean you, you were born here.' And a craven part of my mind will recognise this as an opportunity to demonstrate my values: to define my educated western-ised self as the very opposite to the refugee or the gypsy, to the misplaced and despised. But it is with those people that my sympathies instinctively lie.

So I will overcome this temptation—the temptation to side-step controversy and simply say, 'Well that's alright then'. I will instead want to scream into your smug face: 'But what about my parents? They came here foreign and hopeful, just like the people you hate for begging in the street or forcing down your wages. How can you not get the point?' But I will not do so. I may press for one more conciliatory comment, but at last my expensive, middle-class manners will insist that I acknowledge *their* difficulty. That they are trying to be kind, that they have magnanimously overcome their prejudice and fear to admit me, that I have been given a free pass for one evening at least, and I am expected to be grateful for it. I of course will be left wondering what turn the conversation might have taken had my brown, censoring body not been present at the table.

All these versions of me, the ones reflected back at me from people who feel they are arbiters of what Britishness is, are balanced by the terms of belonging set by other people of colour. Who do I date, black or white men? The answer to this question is the chance for me to gain a stronger toe-hold of belonging to a community of non-white people who struggle to define what 'black' (or Asian, or West Indian, or African...) Britishness is, and where we as individuals fit into ideas of it. I have dated both black and white men, not by conscious choice but based on opportunity: i.e. whoever has bothered to ask me out (score zero points). Is my hair natural or relaxed? Well it is natural (score 10 points) but it is also a very soft afro, very curly rather than hard and kinky (minus 5 points), and so on. It is a game based on a simple template of blackness which the mixed-race person has little hope of neatly fitting.

Most galling of all in this are-you-with-us-or-against-us game of identity Top Trumps, are the white people in love with their own idea of racial difference. They are the ones who express disappointment that I don't speak patois (as if, while kicking around the streets of Leeds, I should have absorbed a form of language to mark my difference, a black-talk to satisfy the white-phobic), are shocked that I am not reggae's most passionate fan, and saddened that I have no desire to sing the blues. Bookish and serious, I am a wigga's worst nightmare and I am most wary of such people: disappoint them and you will be deemed 'ungrateful' or not 'proper' black, by which they mean I, yet again, don't fit their notions of what it is to be non-white, notions that persist almost entirely in the form of stereotypes.

After all, stereotypes render us easy to understand, essentially knowable, predictable—without all that boring business of actually having to get to know us. Again, there is a myth alive here: that the colour of skin *should* mean something. But what? You see, when you mix it up, most ideas of racial identity become meaningless. The race-conscious—by which I mean those who place racial identifications above all others— thrive on the idea that being different must be meaningful; they commonly endow mixed race people with a special status, either that of the multicoloured 'melting pot' dream or of the living evidence of racial dilution. The truth is that we are all and none of these things. We are just us.

These varying gazes, and the demands they make on me, have changed the person I am. I grew up with an awareness that my behaviour must be perfect, because you-know-what would be the reason if I was bad. Shared assumptions and opinions that had nothing to do with me but were always made about me. For instance, that my teeth would be strong, or I could sing, or be good at sport. Later, in the world of work, it would be made known to me that I had been given a chance, hired despite the obvious, therefore I must be more committed, more hardworking. Don't get me wrong—I never had the burning anger of a rebel or revolutionary. But it has stayed alight, a small fire in my belly, bellowed by casual slights, overheard asides and dumb thoughtlessness. I am myself all of the time. But I have to admit, I am also what these people have made me.

If I really must describe the way I look—and I am striving to be accurate—my skin is somewhere between gold and dark mustard. I think of it as a kind of divine brown, which gets an ashy-grey tinge in winter and a deep reddish glow if we have a good summer. Is it a privilege living on the cusp of the colour line, learning to live and love carefully, so that one avoids falling in the cracks? It is a way of life, but was there another way for me? Perhaps I have avoided it or carelessly thrown away my chances for a place of absolute belonging, a place to relax, an alternative to living not on the right side, or on the wrong side, but right on the tracks.

39.
Am I Awake?

I think I'm awake but there is no light. I try to feel my eyelids blink. I concentrate on lifting my eyelids up, feeling them hinge, then setting them down again. I feel them move. I feel a scratchy, dry sensation as they reconnect with the flesh below my eyeball. This flesh exerts a sticky pull as I lift them again. But I cannot see. I reach out with my right hand and come into contact with... what? Smooth dampness. A cool plaster. The chill meeting my fingertips jars with the sensation of damp heat, like a hot towel, that covers the rest of my arm, my shoulder, in fact, my whole body. I am stifled, breathing deliberately through the sodden furnace, expanding my lungs to capture each precious gulp of oxygen. I try to lift my eyelids again, and again the sticky itch of flesh meeting flesh. I stretch out my arm, and again come into contact with the sweaty wall. I press my palm against it. The solidity of the wall presses back.

Palm flat against the wall, I let my eyelids slide shut. The hot towels, where have they come from? I can remember a towel, but it was small, scorching, and...

wrapped in plastic? Behind my closed lids I conjure the fixed, thin line of the girl's mouth as she handed the boiling plastic to me. I'm fairly sure she used an implement, like big tweezers, so she didn't have to touch me or meet my eye. That towel was searing in its heat, but small, like a flannel. Surely not the vast, smothering dampness covering me now. And what is that noise? It sounds like a machine: a regular atonal rhythm singing against the blackness. Not a machine, no... Frogs? Why am I thinking about frogs? Fighting fatigue, I struggle to try and remember: Did someone mention frogs or crickets? But I tire, my thoughts too slow to hold my attention, the darkness too deep, my limbs too heavy. But who has covered me in this... this fine, wet fabric, an ectoplasmic gauze which slides and winds tightly about me as I try to roll onto my side?

It is the pain which forces me to carry on moving. When I try to lift my right leg against the weight of water and cotton, it is the pain which brings it back. I reach down gingerly. My palm, cool from the wall, comes as a small relief for the flesh of my lower leg. I explore it gingerly. The skin is stretched so tight that touching my ankle is as delicate as prodding an over-filled balloon. I guess it to be about twice its normal size. With fingertips light as a dragon-fly's wing, I trace the circumference of my ankle avoiding weeping sores and rubbery coin-sized blisters, yet to burst. And my leg is scorching, hotter even than the shroud wrapping me. I know the heat probably means a raging infection. I relax back onto the bed, for bed I am now sure it is, grateful for the dark and a delay to the sight of the bloated, pussy, mess of a thing hanging from my knee.

With great effort I lift my other arm and sweep cautiously, slowly through the void on my left. I feel the fabric fall away from my wrist, but the atmosphere is still heavy, so that a slow movement is easier in this soupy air and not simply more cautious than a quick one. My hand makes contact with scratchy taut paper. I grope downward, find a spindly metal stem and realise: a lampshade, a lamp base, light. And eventually I find a button which my instinct is to press, but which finally responds to a kind of rocking action.

In the gloomy pool of light, I rest a second, take in my surroundings. My foggy brain recognises the tiny room; its wooden panelled walls, the naive carved wooden crucifix hanging on the wall. The heat beats against the mosquito bites I'd picked up the day before, the very day I'd arrived. I had stood on the edge of an almost-dry river bed, which I now realise could equally have been an open drain, marvelling at the view spread out before me of blue-green sugar-loaf mountains, with a verdant intensity that intimidated as much as it attracted. Each vegetated peak rose narrow and so close to the next that at the sunset, fires were lit on the top of each, a chain of torches glowing welcoming and ominously at the visitor.

I recall that later the previous evening my leg itched. So I took an antihistamine tablet. But sometime in the dark-dark night, the irritated bites turned into a severe allergic reaction to the hungry mosquitoes' kisses, so I had taken more antihistamine, enough to ensure that I would sleep. I hadn't thought of how long it would take me to wake up again. Now the painful itching had turned to swollen, suppurating sores. I had to move, if only to relieve the pressure on my leg. I needed cold wet towels and more drugs, to open the windows and get some air. I had to let Jamaica in.

40.
Miss Julie

I hobble through the heat from downstairs to Miss Julie's kitchen, careful not to knock the balloons of pus that have formed on my leg. Once in the safe, dark kitchen I flop into one of her white plastic chairs and wait for some attention. I have known her less than twenty-four hours but I already know for certain that Miss Julie won't let me down. She is the Don of Black Beach, the queen of this string of white-washed houses. She is light brown with short, copper-coloured hair and wears glasses that hang from her neck down in front of her enormous, unsupported bosom. She is round and loud and likes to cook. She is the kind of woman that I am used to, in a place where there is little I am used to and much I am afraid of. I wait for her to come and observe my suffering.

It is 'up country' here, and far away from the chaos of Kingston. I did not book to stay at Miss Julie's hotel-cum-shop-cum-restaurant, it was just that my original booking had turned out not to be what I expected. It was an apartment which looked fabulous on the internet but when I arrived it was already occupied. First, by a friendly mouse who came out to see who the interloper was. The mouse was then followed by ants, marching confidently in two lanes across my bed. Then there was the frog who popped his green head up out of the shower's filthy plughole, eyeing the pinkish, no-skin coloured lizards which clung to the mildewed wall. I killed the first huge cockroach which ambled, amiably enough across the sooty lino from behind the recession-era Frigidaire. But there was, it seemed, an unseen army of cockroaches, because as I killed one, they sent another giant armour-plated reconnaissance bug out, then another.

The taxi driver, my rescuer, suggested Miss Julie's. Miss Julie took me and my belongings in like a red cross volunteer accepting a refugee. I was immediately comforted by her house: the ground floor had a small shop which served customers from a window at the side. Every kind of everyday need could be met from the shelves and fridges of Miss Julie's store: beer, plasters, pain killers, biscuits, baked goods, crisps and, of course, chicken and rice cooked in her cool, spotless kitchen. She had a particularly good assortment of cleaning products: Ajax, Quix, Fabuloso, Super Brite, Mr Sheen, Palmolive. Giant chest freezers in the back held cuts of meat and fish, while beside them stood industrial-sized vats of chemicals specifically for keeping the guest rooms upstairs free of non-human life. On her porch, a small group of men sat, and while sitting swapped cigarettes and gossip. I felt I had arrived at the home of a particularly sociable and hygiene-conscious auntie.

Miss Julie was a woman who liked to feed people and I am a woman who likes to eat. Within a few hours I had returned to my natural childhood state: I had been adopted by a kind stranger, I was appreciatively wolfing down her food, basking in her benign gaze. Although in truth, our conversation didn't flow immediately. Until I'd got used to her accent—much stronger than those I'd heard in Kingston or Ocho Rios, and much stronger than any I'd heard in Yorkshire—I just smiled and nodded through mouthfuls. And fortunately, Miss Julie didn't wait for replies.

I show her my ruined leg and she takes a long, serious, satisfying look at it and kisses her teeth and makes a long low sound, half-groan and half-whistle.

"You got de oin-ment? You wanna be byin ointment!" I explained I had a range of tablets, creams, and repellents and none of it had saved me.

"Wat yo wan? A mek ya chicken. Me chicken fay-mus. Sit dere."

She knew better than I that food was the answer, so I sat. And after a while Miss Julie, if she had no customers, would lean against the shop counter while I ate, perhaps letting the hams of her forearms rest against the giant ledger in which she carefully noted every debt, large and small, her customers owed. She would lean and reminisce and I would sit and eat.

"Ya naa doll-sis?"

"Doll sis? Oh yes! Dolcis. It's a shoe shop!"

And after a short time I stopped having to check my interpretation, and my ears became accustomed to the rhythm and cadences of her speech.

"That's right. That's where I work. Long time now. On Oxford Street. You know Abba-van. All the soil?"

She pronounced it 'serl' but I couldn't get what Abba had to do with it. But munching on the cold, tasty fried chicken gives me thinking time until the light-bulb comes on.

"Aberfan. I think I've heard about it. It was a slag heap that collapsed on top of a school. A big disaster. Was it in the sixties?"

"Yeah. While I work at Dol-cis. Was so sad. All them pickney." The low groaning, whistling sound again while she thinks about the disaster and then asks me how well I know London.

In this way our conversation moves me forward through the days. The bites on my leg start to heal and I begin to notice more of what is happening around me. My respect for Miss Julie grows: everybody knows her, and no one disrespects her. And there is nothing that she doesn't know: she is at the centre of the delicate chains—kindness, credit and a belief in the divine—which bind this small hamlet of souls. A place where there was little to do, where distance was measured in 'chains', where I could cower under Miss Julie's protection forever.

I would love to stay wrapped up in the warmth of

Miss Julie, but I have a sense of quiet urgency pressing on my mind. A spectre haunted my peripheral vision, it was only a vague outline. A vague outline of the thing I told myself I wasn't looking for, the thing I hadn't flown thousands of miles to discover. It took me longer than it should have to face up to my hopes. I happened to glance at a telephone book and realised there couldn't be more than a couple of hundred of the surname 'Anglin' listed. That was my Daddy's surname. The kernel of an idea began to pierce my denial: perhaps there was someone left? Someone who knew him? I had looked for smaller needles in much bigger haystacks, but the prize then was never so dear.

41.

Another Ending

In the mid-1980s, just as Aristotle's was taking off, my school career came to an end. For other members of the family a new page turned too. Andrew has been married for a few years now and has been posted by the army to Paderborn in Germany for years, rather than months, this time. I am on the phone to him as he describes every detail of his new baby girl.

"...Her hands are so tiny, but the nails are all perfect. And her little eyes are covered by her minute eyelashes. Her feet..." I roll my eyes with endearment, while Andrew continues telling me about how exquisite his daughter is.

It is the Autumn of my sixteenth year and I am living with Mam full time. While she works downstairs, I continue to spend too many long hours in my room. But now I am attending the local tech to do my A levels (though attendance is not something I've yet realised is necessary in order to pass). I am intoxicated with freedom: to wake up and go to bed pretty much when I please. To get a job, to drink out in town with the few friends in Leeds I've managed to hang on to. There is a fancy-dress party at my new college tonight and me and a friend are skipping yet another class to go into town and visit Hombergs, the theatrical costumiers, to choose our outfits. I am keen to go as an old-fashioned French can-can girl, but first I must find out if a brown, over-weight sixteen-year-old can dress-up as a can-can girl and get away with it.

Mam is busy with her own work and the business. Aristotle's is doing well. We are living well, I think. Well, Mam asked me if I wanted to return to school for my 'A' levels, so she must have the money. I turned the question over and over in my mind all summer: the case in favour of returning is strong. By early August I knew I had passed eleven of the 12 'O' levels I entered. This was good news in the family: everyone was sure I was destined for academic greatness. Only Paul was different, he was very quiet when I went round to tell him. He knitted his eyebrows together and turned the corners of his mouth downward, in an expression I always associate with him. It was a look of puzzled loss, of one who is thwarted without quite knowing how or why.

It's clear that I could go back to boarding school and expect to do well, but the case against returning is even stronger: I am sick of the regime at school: the idea of a social life which consists of people I have lived with, eaten with and played with for the last four years is unut-terably dull. Education is important, I know this, it has been drilled into me, but what about music, drinking and friends? As the summer turned cool, Mam accepted my decision to do 'A' levels in Leeds with equanimity. I think she's pleased to be shot of the fees.

But this means I am around all the time, and we are not coping well with our new arrangement. I am not the twelve-year-old who went away to school and there have been many rows. Arguments which soon become screaming matches, and when I quickly forget why we are arguing and give in to my anger, enjoying it for its own sake. In fact, today, we are making an effort to be nice to each, so after going into town for our costumes, I am going to meet Mam. She has a ballroom dancing lesson at Dennis Altman's dancing school behind the Town Hall and after she is done we are going out for something to eat. Mam is out when I leave, probably at the sauna, but I know she has been a bit a worried and needs cheering up.

Typically, Paul is the focus of her fretting. Yesterday he borrowed her new car, telling her he needed it to drive to an interview at a school in Boston Spa. Paul is working as a caretaker at a college in Horsforth. He hates his job, we know, and he can't really bear to be around the students, who can sense in him something fragile. They have made his job difficult, he tells us. They go out of their way to walk across a floor he has just mopped. They shout things at him, or whisper under their breaths just out of earshot.

I mention to my friend how odd it is that Paul hasn't brought the car back on time. He wasn't supposed to keep it overnight and he hasn't phoned. "But a bit of me thinks, good on you. I wonder if he's just driven off to start a new life, and if he has I'm pleased for him," I tell my mate, still drunk on my own liberty.

We have picked our outfits for the party now, the showgirl ones really looked great and had feathers and everything, and they even had one to fit me. My mate has taken them home to her house where we are going to get ready together, so I leave her in town and walk down The Headrow toward the Town Hall. I arrive just as Mam's private lesson with Lilly is due to end. I like Lilly, she is a very tall, very elegant old lady—at least 60—who always wears her custard-coloured hair up in an immaculate chignon. I like watching her dance with Mam who is about a foot shorter than her but nearly as elegant when they both spin around the parquet floor doing the cha-cha-cha.

I climb happily up the steep stairs which lead to Altman's ballroom and peer around the door but Mam isn't there. There isn't even any music. The huge room is deserted apart from Lilly who, when she notices me, looks at me hard, almost like she's never seen me before, so I smile at her to remind her of who I am. But she doesn't smile back, and the atmosphere in the empty ballroom is full of her fear. I can feel it radiating from her lean body, I can almost taste it. She walks towards me silently, and then leads me by the elbow to one of the chairs pushed around the side of the dance floor.

"What's the matter? Tell me!" I ask repeatedly, for her fear has made me frightened. Eventually she says: "Your mum phoned, she said something had happened to her son."

"What happened? What happened?"

"She said it was serious."

After that, time falls away. Lilly and another woman are speaking in loud, stagy whispers and there is an arm around me, but I just want to get home to find out what's happened.

And then I am home and find Mam in the front room, there are other people there but I can't focus on them, I can only look at Mam. I know from my first glance at her that it is Paul. It is, after all, always Paul. Except this time, he will not be coming back.

"Paul's dead," she says and wraps her arms around me. And just like that, my world shatters before I feel the first of many hot tears run down my face.

42.

The Business of Death

In the wake of a tragedy it is extraordinary how quickly the administrative business of death must be attended to, arrangements must be made, the proper authorities must be informed, people must be told. It seems that Mam has been trying to get hold at me at college, unaware that I had skipped classes. Now I am home, she leaves me. Someone must identify Paul's body, and as he was found deep in the Yorkshire countryside, she has a bit of a journey ahead of her. Somehow I must have volunteered, or been volunteered, to phone Andrew in Germany and tell him about his brother's death.

I remember the call. Not what was said, but the awareness that I was about to drive a tank through my soldier-brother's new-born happiness. In his voice I heard the bitterness of loss lean in on his vocal chords. His voice was accepting but had fallen to a lower register. Unlike me, he had experienced sudden death before when his father had been killed. I think he told me he would fly back as soon as he could, but instead of listening to his words, I was caught up trying to gain some comfort, trying to feel my big brother's calm deep voice spread like a balm over my distress.

A few hazy days later, Andrew has flown back and we attend the inquest. It is a formal, dignified process. Seriously, everyone should have one. There are official types who speak with voices weighed down by gravitas. There is no doubt. There is a note, the locked car doors, the grey and grieving relatives. I notice a middle-aged man there, noting everything down. I thought he must have been part of the coroner's staff, but actually he was a journalist. The headline was 'Tragedy at Beauty Spot'.

An assistant caretaker who worried about his work borrowed his mother's car and killed himself with the exhaust fumes at a Dales beauty spot, an inquest heard.

The body of Paul Nicholas Massey, 25, was found at Deepdale, near Buckden, last Thursday.

A pipe connected to the exhaust led inside the vehicle and Mr Massey had left a note on the dashboard indicating he intended to take his own life.

Mrs Michelle Massey told the Harrogate inquest her husband took great pride in his work at a college at Horsforth, Leeds, but easily became depressed. He had said he was going to look at a school at Boston Spa where there was a vacancy.

The Claro Coroner, Dr Sidney Jacobs, recorded a verdict that Mr Massey killed himself while suffering from depression.

It had happened like this; Paul had borrowed my Mam's car on the pretext of going to an interview. In fact, he drove to a well-known local beauty spot with a length of hose. He attached the hose to the exhaust before putting the other end of the hose inside his mouth and taping it closed. He'd placed a suicide note on the dashboard to ensure it would be found along with his body. In the note he said he was happy to be going to a place where the pain he felt would be over. He told me, my mum and Michelle, his wife of less than two years, that he loved us. On the reverse of the note was a diagram of the car, the pipe from the exhaust, what he planned to do. So he didn't really give an explanation, and even today, when I am asked why he did it, I have no clear reason to give.

The next time I saw Paul he was lying in the Co-op Funeral Service's Chapel of Rest. I didn't want to walk into the dimly lit municipal building. Encouragement flowed from Andrew, his assurances that it would be fine, that it was better to go through with it than not, that there was nothing to be scared of. So much so, that I still wonder how he was able to show such courage.

Andrew's baby girl was just a few weeks old. In that telephone conversation only days before I had listened to a different man. A man elated by his new daughter's perfection, obsessed with her minuteness: her tiny nails, the curve of her still-soft skull. Then I had to phone him and tell him Paul had killed himself and that Mam had gone to identify the body. And now a haggard and grieving Andrew was trying to persuade his little sister to view the body of his dead brother.

With his encouragement I stepped into the Chapel of Rest and, averting my eyes, joined Andrew beside the coffin. I took a second to steel myself then I focussed clearly on Paul. What I saw nearly made me laugh out loud. There he was, lying in an expensive and too-shiny wooden box covered with a white, lacy sheet thing, only his head exposed. His face was made-up so he looked more deeply tanned than I'd ever seen him. On his usually grumpy, down-turned mouth, a gentle smile played on his too-red lips. Even his then-fashionable moustache was neatly trimmed. This thing looked totally unlike anyone I had known.

I later found that the dark, American-tan make up was a necessity because of the carbon monoxide poisoning which turned Paul's flesh blue-black. I understood that the ambulance staff had probably had to break his jaw to remove the plastic tubing, so it was likely his cadaver had small wooden posts inside the lips supporting the mouth and this was the closest they could get to a natural expression. The autopsy and the circumstances of his death had made dressing the body difficult, hence the obscuring shroud. In fact, much less than three quarters of him was probably in the box. The rest I imagine stayed at the teaching hospital, resting in jars on a consultant's mahogany desk. "And this is the effect of massive doses of carbon monoxide gas on the major organs..." he would say year after year to cynical, seen-it-all, medical students. What was left of Paul, his human remains, was only the approximation of a person, a near-miss at best. In a different context I would have thought it a grossly over-sized ventriloquist's doll with a passing resemblance to my brother.

After this revelation, the funeral itself took on a weird, masked ball-like quality. We, the family, stood outside Paul's house in a murmur of black. The serious, all-male staff from the undertakers carried wreaths from the house with both hands and a kind of self-important precision. They then placed them in the hearse carrying Paul's coffin. Their slightly shiny Victorian frock-coats brought to mind churchyard crows. When this was done, Mam, Andrew, Michelle and I squashed into the back of an elderly black Daimler to travel behind the hearse. In this uncomfortable state, and forced to stare at the box containing my brother's corpse, we made our way at about ten miles an hour the few miles from Headingly to Lawnswood Crematorium.

We were quite a show. As we made our way at a glacial pace through the busy Saturday morning traffic, by passers casually walked alongside the hearse, trying to take a peak. Older women especially glared at us with lurid fascination. It wasn't long before Andrew said something about the ludicrousness of our situation and the heightened hysteria in the vehicle meant that we began giggling. We each tried to hide it at first, but a strangled yelp here and a shaking shoulder there meant that soon we were all off. Tears of anger and grief streaked our faces while mouths gasped for air and cheeks ached. The more hypnotised our audience, the more we laughed. The driver stayed calm as we, inappropriate mourners, guffawed and shook in the back seats.

By the time we arrived at the Crematorium we were exhausted—there was nothing left of us but tears. I cried all the way through the service and the next thing I knew the hideous carcass in its ugly box was gone, along with the vestiges of our family life.

The administrative stuff of death, its practicalities and demands were over. It was only the beginning for us of course and even now, we do not discuss these events. The courage we had all shown then seems to have deserted us, drained away like adrenaline after a race.

43.
The View from Here

I left Miss Julie and my trip settled back into the steps I had carefully planned out before leaving England. It is a shock to be somewhere and not feel black, which is not to say that I fit in here.

I left Miss Julie to stay in a small, luxury resort I had pre-booked. It is beautiful: a stunning confection. Camden market-like, the place hums with the variety of aqua, emerald green, turquoise and peach-coloured hand-painted decoration (both inside and outside), all executed on a vaguely nautical theme. It is like walking through a dry tropical fish tank. Here, other people like me, by which I mean tourists, fall into conversation with carefully-vetted 'locals', Jamaicans who will sit with you for the price of a drink or a meal and in their aimless but pretty chatter give the visitor an authentic experience. They are, in fact, almost employees. They lack none of Aunt Julie's business skills and practical good sense: but they have a more disturbing quality—they make me feel rich.

These men, and it always is men, speak to me like

poets. I ask one, a chef at Pelican Reef, a shack on stilts I am visiting which is stranded out at sea and accessible only by boat, if he is lonely at his isolated station. "Lonely...?" he ruminates. "Nobody has ever asked me that... Yes. I am lonely. I am an Adam waiting for his Eve." I am charmed until, a couple of minutes later, an attractive young woman arrives in a small launch, his lunch in her hands.

Poverty was everywhere, but so was hope, faith in God and an unshakable commitment to Jamaica's extraordinary cultural achievements. In the early afternoon, I looked forward to the sight of schoolchildren with smiles as white as their shirts, released from school and larking around before disappearing into their wonky tin shacks. As someone pointed out to me: Is there anyone who hasn't heard of Jamaica? The other tourists we met complained of hustlers who will sell you anything and will do most things for a dollar or two and declare their undying love in hope of a passport. But, I argued, it's an understandable ambition, escaping from this paradise, and many pursue it with verbal dexterity and charisma.

With my clothes, car and hair I stand out like a sore thumb. 'Hey red!' the beach boys called, or sometimes 'Yo, Yellow!' So here, I am not black, but I am still coloured. I am yellow or red. I am also rich. And it is the wealth of my advantages, the most particular one it seems being the freedom to leave, which presses on me here. Thinking about this, I fall into conversation with

Jason, who runs the resort with his Aunt, June. I tell them about my father, and they ask questions. And while I hope that their questions wouldn't lead anywhere, I also hoped they would say something like: "Oh yes, we knew the Anglins..."

Instead, Jason tells me to follow him. He takes me to a kind of open-air office area, picks up the telephone receiver and phone book and puts them down in front of me as if telling me to get on with it. "But I might have to make dozens of calls..." I argue, looking his gift horse squarely in the mouth. "That's OK. Just let me know when you've finished." And he leaves me there with the tools of excavating my past, one I knew nothing about. I find I can't refuse his kindness, so nervously, I open the phone book to the less-than-a-page of Jamaican Anglins, plant my left-hand forefinger firmly under the first entry and begin to dial.

On the phone, I discovered that Jamaica is indeed a small island. When I phone one Anglin in one particular Parish, I would soon be talking to their relatives in the same parish. Most people were kind but dismissive—I was trying to sound friendly and not at all the type of person that Cyril Anglin might have lent money to, so they had no easy excuse to just put the phone down. Nevertheless, some did. A few were lovely. The magnificently named Byron Anglin pointed out that I was probably related to him anyway, even if we couldn't work out exactly how, and I must come for a visit to his home in

Montego Bay. A nice thought but right now I had a list of calls to make. Perhaps I would find my father's children, two half-brothers I half-knew existed? What if I only came across a cousin, even second or third? Well, that would be fine, as long as they could tell me something about my dad.

I carried on phoning, but realising it was a waste of time to call every Anglin in every parish, I began picking only a couple from each. I soon came to a dead end. Even among the people who couldn't understand my accent, or whose accent I couldn't follow, it was clear from the pauses they took or the immediacy of their loud "Who?" that they'd never heard of a Cyril Anglin. Some told me that I'd just spoken to their sister, or aunt, or mother, and no, they didn't know any Cyril either. My final attempt was to call the radio station, as I'd been told that on a Sunday evening there was a show where people would advertise their searches for relatives. I called them, and they were polite, but Sunday was still days away. When the evening came I sat by the radio and waited. But there was nothing. It was as I had feared: Daddy had come to Britain with his siblings, and without them there was no one who remembered him.

When my final morning arrived I was asked to join Jason, June and the staff for their morning prayers. Being a non-believer, I found their faith and their desire to share it with me intensely touching. Their short gathering was bitter sweet for me: I envied their certitude and calm acceptance, both qualities that I lacked. Still, I couldn't get with the God part, I, whose silent secular prayer had remained so resolutely unanswered. My thoughts turned to home, another small island that had become more vivid and distinct the further I fled. It is time for me to go home.

It is clear to me now, during the quiet murmur of private prayers, that I do love my country. I do not wish to be elsewhere. I will board the plane back to my island of shrugs and turned backs, dry stone walls and winter fogs, drizzle and summer lightning. For it is home. So yes, I do love my country. It is just that I am not sure if she loves me.

44.
After All

Received wisdom has it that after everyone has left the wake, the hangovers are healed, the glasses are polished and returned to their shelves, the flowers have wilted and the undertakers' invoice paid, only then does the private process of mourning for loved ones begin. This order of events applies if the bereaved are people for whom death creates a space to nurture relationships with others who loved the departed. I believe there are such people: I have read about them in books. But it may not be like this.

Alternatively, after the public ceremonies, the long goodbyes, the fond dabbing of eyes, it may be different for another type of person, a type of girl perhaps not so schooled in the proper way to do things, perhaps one who to protect herself from a harshness that already existed, hung on to her childish imagination longer than was wise. Perhaps for such a person it may be easier and cosier to believe that it has all been some kind of pantomime; that the players will shed their ghostly makeup, wipe their cheeks free of streaked mascara, and go back to the real world, by which I mean the world as it was before.

The sixteen-year-old me waited for this innocent state of pre-knowledge to return, I didn't know that what I learned from Paul's short life could not be unlearned, that simply ignoring our failure to save him wouldn't make him come back. But what could have enabled the water of time to close over the wound of his death, so that the idea of us three as a family could be reconstructed from the shattered people who remained?

Andrew returned to his life, with his wife and new daughter. He was never so involved with us again, never so close to our dramas, which continued of course, because a death is never really a full-stop, it just feels like it.

Now it was just me and Mam, eyeball to eyeball, constantly followed by the infinite sadness of what had happened. Mam didn't talk, and she coped in her style, but the grief came out anyway. At times she was unable to swallow her own saliva and would have to dab away at her mouth with a handkerchief. She would cry at the slightest mention of his name. She would cry, too, when there was no mention of his name. Gradually, I fell under similar spells. I got the same swallowing condition: a billiard ball hung in my throat, ready to suffocate me. The result of the physical manifestation of all that could not be discussed. So I plotted to leave the house, and her, as quickly as decently possible. By the time spring arrived, Mam had agreed to pay the rent on a bedsit for me while I took my A levels. This freed me from her unspoken anguish, so with an ease made from terror, I quit 24 Victoria Park Avenue, and never lived there again. And, though we were never out of telephone touch for long, Mam and I were not to spend any significant amount of time together under the same roof for more than two decades.

This is how suicide destroys a family. It happens gradually almost like a cancer. It starts small. Each member appears to absorb the shock of the beloved's death, but inevitably the individuals are distorted by the event in unique ways. The grief works its way outward, like a piece of bone trapped in soft tissue. The body is unaware of the splinter gradually working its way through layers of flesh, until one day a harsh edge begins to emerge, an incongruous shard jutting out from soft skin.

Why did we pull away from each other, rather than draw closer around the object of our obsession? I suspect we did it to protect ourselves from the temptation to explore questions which have no answers. The pain. The endless uncertainty of if Paul could have been convinced out of his terminal state of mind. If we could have guessed at his intentions, if we had just spotted the signs, if he could have become a more resilient man, if he'd had the chance. At twenty-five, was it possible for him to have known himself? Was it possible for him to have made a decision that was not only right for him then, but also right for the rest of time?

And perhaps we do it to protect the version of Paul we

choose to remember, the version that allows us to nurture him dead, as we never got the chance to in life. Have I told you about the brother I know now, the one who was so musical he could hear a song once then play it back to you? Who was a natural on any kind of keyboard, who played the organ to rooms full of people with pure ease and not one ounce of showmanship. In this version, the elements of his personality that pushed him to the end of his life have receded and I am free to remember the good in him, the unexpected smile, the curiosity, those green eyes. The hard shell I have built around these memories protects me much more than it protects Paul because he is in no further need of it.

But perhaps I am being romantic, because grief sits easily with swooning, and purple prose and rose-tinted half-lies. The last time I saw Paul was in a dream. I am sat on the stairs of 24 Victoria Park Avenue. I am an adult, sitting on the stairs in my nightie, the sun not yet set, listening to what is happening behind the living room door, wondering if I dare go in when I should be in bed—I am sat like this, in a state of anticipation, when Paul walks in through the front door. And he stands in the hall beneath me, smiling at me, as if he's just come in from buying fags at the corner shop.

"Are you OK?" I ask him.

"Yes," he grins.

"Well, I'm glad you are!" I shout. I stand and turn my back to him, fleeing up the stairs to the safety of my rose-patterned bedroom, knowing that even years after the tragedy of his death, I can't really forgive him.

So this is the way you found us. These hard shards, of anger, lack of care, guilt, love wasted, love lost have had years to do their work and they are numerous, as abundant as memories. Each works its way through the psyche, toughening and changing their host. Like a hammer resounding on a drum, bouncing off the skin repeatedly until the once-taut leather loses its facility to absorb the impact and begins to sag. Such was the effect of our grief. Like very gradual weight loss, the changes were invisible to Mam, to Andrew, to me, until, years later we would look at each other and no longer properly recognise the people we saw.

45.
The Way We Live Now

I am sitting in this pine and bleach smelling cupboard-room because I feel guilty. I feel guilty a lot these days, and often the circumstances which arise from these emotions directly benefit Mam. I don't know how she does it. How does she get these feelings out of me?

As a result, on this dank Wednesday morning, I was riding in a taxi with Mam rather than tackling the work that squats on my desk. Mam was in a good mood, the atmosphere in the taxi was one of anticipation, like we could be on a daytrip to the coast rather than visiting the hospital radiologist. We chatted to the taxi driver about our part of Leeds and its wealthy residents, and their innate suspicion of anything new, and whether or not our little row of shops could support an Indian restaurant.

"Businesses are always opening and closing around here. I think someone tried before but everyone complained about the smell," explained Mam.

And my eyes met the driver's in his rear view mirror, a long-enough glance which made clear we both understood that this was a kind of code, and that it was the restauranteurs' race, rather than their food, which had offended.

On arrival, I was offended by the sleek purposeful-ness and brand new-ness of the reception area. There were waiting chairs, thoughtfully laid out in a socially cohesive semi-circle before us, and bolted to the floor so they could not be moved for the purposes of conversation or comfort. The huge hexagonal desk of simulated wood, the pale green walls, are clearly designed according to a text book about how to treat ill people, and Mam is not ill, I am sure, she is just old. At the desk we were greeted by a middle-aged woman with back-combed blonde hair who kindly asked us to wait and sit on one of the bolted chairs, before pointing us out to a nurse. She was pleas-ant and efficient—I searched hard for offence, but there was none to be taken.

So now we are waiting, and waiting, among the old, and those who look old because they are so ill, and those who slowly sip water from plastic cups between pain-laden breaths. When the nurse bustles over, she is smiling broadly and is clearly going to be lovely to my Mam and I am relieved. Mam would not be expecting anything less. The nurse acknowledges me, but peers down to her and indulgently makes proper eye contact. She talks much more loudly to Mam than she does to me.

"Is this your mother?" the nurse asks me.

"Yes" I reply.

"HELLO MRS MASSEY," the nurse bellows to my

mother, who actually isn't that deaf, but never minds.

"Hello. We had a lovely taxi ride here. The driver was really interesting," informs my Mam.

Then to me: "She's here for radiology is she?"

"Yes."

"Can you take her to that room over there?" The nurse asks me, then says to Mam:

"THAT'S NICE LOVE. JUST GO TO THAT ROOM OVER THERE MRS MASSEY AND WAIT FOR ME."

She doesn't wait for Mam to reply, even though her instructions are perfectly simple, and I want to shout at her that Mam is old, but not an imbecile. Instead I hurry Mam off, though really we achieve a kind of slow shuffle, in the direction of the radiology theatre.

I am annoyed with the nurse—finally something to get frustrated about—but I know it's not her fault, and my little furious balloon quickly deflates. Everybody checks, and it is fine, it really is. After all, in their eyes I could more easily be this elderly white woman's carer than her daughter. Mam is always telling people (in the cafe at Debenhams, on the bus) "This is my daughter," before they ask, or show any interest at all. For years I thought it was because she was particularly proud of me. Now, in these hospital days, I know it is also because she doesn't want them to think she needs professional help.

Far from minding the nurse's unnecessary indulgence of her non-deafness, her attention has a regressive effect on Mam. So that when we get to the tiny anteroom where she must undress, there is nothing of the fearsome woman I am used to. She has become smaller in front of my eyes, grinning like a child, cheerfully offering me part of the tiny narrow bench to sit on, peering around at the cell-like space.

"Sit here Kate. Fold my things as I take them off? There's not enough room to swing Monty in here."

"If there was room to swing Monty, we'd be going private." And we laugh.

She is clearly happy to be prodded, grabbed, jabbed, and photographed by these professionally caring women. She is perhaps even looking forward to it. Care is something that she happily accepts from strangers.

In the radiology theatre's tiny anteroom, Mam begins to remove her layers of clothing. Foremost is the padded, cream anorak, her first defence against the blustery Yorkshire breeze. Then comes off a bright sunset-pink cardigan with sequins around the neck. Next a long sleeved black cotton top, which she lifts from the hem, and unpeels a small degree from her body. But she begins to struggle like an escapologist in a straitjacket. I lift my hands, palms up, to offer my help but, I hope, without suggesting she can't do it herself. Before my raised hands, she stops struggling and rests. She says nothing to indicate I should move toward her, merely looks down, but I take her stillness as acquiescence and gently loose the fabric from her stubby fingers. I draw the top up, covering her face for a moment, shroud-like, before cautiously lifting it over her sparse white scalp and clear of her head.

She now sits in a black vest and knickers, a black and cream shadow of her clothed self. Despite the hated crepe skin on her upper arms being on display, she relaxes, taking a long moment to undo the suspenders holding up her thick black stockings. She rolls one stocking down and then another as close to the end of her feet as she can, before reaching creakily forward for the tip of each one and plucking it free of her foot. The vest is easy, she slips down the straps from each shoulder, then, leaning forward to stand, she places a steadying hand on the pale green paintwork. She uses the other hand to work the vest, suspender belt and knickers gathered about her waist downward toward the ground in a single piece.

All that remains is her bra, which has ground its way into her white flesh, so that, when she reaches around to unhook the clasp, angry red binds are revealed at her shoulders. As she removes it, her pale puckered breasts drip from their cups into my eye line. I think, this small round, balding woman, aged but somehow ageless like a full moon, is a stranger to me. But with the certainty of time I am aware that I will grow to know her intimately. The thought inflates my fury. I am ensnared again by guilt, am angry that she is so vulnerable, am ashamed of my anger. In this state, too young to be her parent and too old to be her child, I am useless to her. I turn to unhook the waiting gown, rather than look.

46.
Atonement

We are watching a movie together, not something we do often these days: Mam's concentration is beginning to desert her. Where once she read books, devouring a Martina Cole or Mary Wesley in a day or two, now she makes do with magazines and the *Yorkshire Evening Post*. This is her currency now—short news pieces, letters to the editor, gossip packaged as articles for the over fifties. Instead of the Saturday matinee musicals of my girlhood we have *Strictly Come Dancing* and *Come Dine With Me*. These shows give us time in the moment to enjoy ourselves without the shadow of the past, they even give us a small future to look forward to—who will win? Who will be sent home this week?

For this visit I didn't have very far to come. In fact, I only came down the stairs. Because now, after running so hard to get away from her, I literally live on top of her. We have bought a house and split it into two. She has the ground floor, and I live upstairs. We have our own self-contained flats with two separate doors in the shared hall, which are good for when we are not speaking. It has taken twenty-odd years for me and Mam to achieve our uneasy truce, but we have crossed the Rubicon on the sail of the stories we tell each other, borne by oars of pragmatism. I accept that I am her daughter, and I accept I am what she has made me. I accept that she is now too old for me to easily leave again.

So this sitting down together and watching a film is unusual, but I thought she might like it. It is *Atonement* and because it is a tragic romance and set in the Second World War it seems appropriate: not so different in setting and subject matter from the last film we watched together: *The End of the Affair*. Even *Waterloo Bridge* is similar: Young, beautiful people are thwarted in their attempts at happiness, then someone dies. Just the ticket.

So we settle down in her new front room: it is decorated in an up-to-the-minute combination of duck-egg blue and brown with chintzy wallpaper, a new striped armchair and a special bed for Monty. He is seventeen now, and when I come into the living room he habitually awakes, stares at me with gimlet eyes and leaps heftily onto Mam's lap, and she pushes him off before he settles cosily into her side, paws tucked neatly under, purring like a traction engine. His marmalade head rubs her forearm until he gets the attention he craves. Mam's babyish scratching, stroking and coochy-cooing belie Monty's great age. And, though he hasn't lost an ounce of weight, he sleeps nearly all the time now, waking briefly to eat, or when there's a visitor to whom he can demonstrate his superiority, and these days, that visitor is usually me.

I operate the DVD player, a piece of technology which has come too late for my mother to learn her way around. The film starts and now we can concentrate on it, rather than each other, and live our experience of the movie as it unfolds. A fresh thing, a new thing for us to obsess over, dissect and criticise. There are fewer and fewer new things these days. We talk about my brother and his family, my dog, Monty, our flats, work that needs doing on the house. But more and more, though the conversation starts in the present, we are inevitably drawn backward in time. My mother will often begin to tell me, say, about the telephone conversation she has just had with Andrew, before she drifts into recounting a past memory. And more and more these memories are the same ones over and over again. But I just listen, I will always listen.

The beautiful pictures unfold: the country mansion, the wood-panelled corridors, the manicured lawns, the aristocrats choreographed through them like formation dancers. And a strange thing happens: Mam and I are silent. Instead of our usual running commentary on the dresses, the music, the interiors, we are quiet. We are silent through the absurd country-house accents, Keira Knightley's thinness—so extreme that I can't tell from her body if she is facing the camera or glancing over a bony shoulder, which she does a lot—and a plot which rests on nobody ever sitting down and having a proper conversation. We are silent through the tragedy that unfolds because it is about what is said, and what remains unsaid, and so, it is about us and we have run out of words.

Tears are running down my face now. To soaring strings, an injured James McAvoy surveys the beach at Dunkirk with red-rimmed eyes. It was a pleasure beach, and though the big wheel still turns, it has become a ruined garrison of three hundred thousand stranded men. Men shooting their horses as a kindness, men with their eyes trained on the watery horizon singing out their sorrows. "Dear Lord and Father of mankind, forgive our foolish ways." Men drinking, men going mad, men dying, dogs running in packs and feasting on the carcasses. And I forget the film as I wonder who my mother sees on the screen. The Grandfather she never knew who died in the first war? Her son surveying the beaches of the Malvinas for Argentine enemies? Or her father, the airman, the adventurer who returned? On the screen, our hero's wound has become infected and blood poisoning takes hold before he can be evacuated. It is as McAvoy sweatily breathes his last that Mam breaks our silence.

"No wonder my Dad kept going on about his foot," she says, without particular emphasis or excitement.

"What do you mean?"

"Your grandfather was there," she gestures toward the screen with her tea-cup. "He walked eight miles without a gun. He was Airforce, so they didn't have guns."

It takes a minute for me to drag myself out of the film and bring to mind my Granddad Horace, another teller of interminable stories. But this was new: I didn't know Granddad had been rescued from Dunkirk, was part of the body of men transported by small boats back to England and safety.

"He walked to Dunkirk?"

"Oh me and my brother used to get sick of hearing him go on about it. He'd have all the crockery and lay it out. The salt would be one village, the pepper the beach and his knife and fork would be the Germans. Kept going on about a sore he had on his foot. I see why now. Must have been scared."

And just like that, the past opens up again like a wormhole in the middle of Mam's beige-and-chocolate rug. As the credits roll on the screen, Mam stabs the remote control trying to get programmes back on and Monty snores gently under the movie's sobbing piano strings, a welter of history bears down on us again. We are an ordinary mother with her ordinary daughter, each made out of the other, sat in this blue and brown room. And I want our newly precious, but vague currents of understanding to tow us into a kind of present. A place where we can consider not only the vast losses we have suffered, but also what we still have to gain. But with this new disclosure I feel our relationship's shallow foundations shudder a little as they shift to accommodate another new story, another little tile settling in our family mosaic. But with each adjustment, each cloud of newly disturbed certainties, I have lost some of the will to fight.

I admit it, I have grown weak. In the family ledger I can neither credit nor discount this new revelation, and for the first time, I do not want to. I am worn out by infesting lies, the repeated assaults of all the dramas that have gone before, all the turmoil we have journeyed through. My muscles are atrophied, the tactics of my youth redundant. I am no longer the keeper of secrets because I am not fit for the job. Now, head bowed, trudging into Mam's diminishing future, I find I cannot resist the torrent of her words heaving us back into the past. A contested past, of course, one on which we will never quite agree, which I can never entirely trust to be true, but one which is still a kind of home.

Acknowledgments

For support along the way my gratitude to Kit de Waal, Unbound, and the Common People authors who have become friends, Professor Bernardine Evaristo, MBE, Linda Anderson, Jack Mapanje, Crista Ermiya, Dawn Cameron, Blake Morrison, Jacob Ross, The SI Leeds Literary Prize, Lesley Wood and everyone at New Writing South, Inscribe and ACE England.

I am appreciative of the team at Jacaranda, who's commitment to seeing stories like mine make it out into the world has been awe-inspiring. I am very proud to be selected as one of their twenty new authors of colour.

My friends have looked, laughed, wondered and occasionally despaired along with me. I am thankful for them all and especially Sylvia Mead and Mel Gebler for their unwavering optimism and encouragement, while Graham Welch and Damon Biddlecombe kept my glass overflowing and the tears at bay.

Love and gratitude to my family, especially Yvette who lived it all and shared her life so generously, Eve, Gary Scott (who probably knows this text by heart) and Genevieve Joy Scott-Massey who will, I hope, one day be proud of it.

About the Author

Katy Massey grew up in Yorkshire and was as a free-lance journalist for 15 years. *Are We Home Yet?* formed the creative element of her PhD in memoir and auto-biography, awarded by Newcastle University in 2010. Her research informed her recent work as a project producer and editor focussed on sourcing and publishing life stories which may otherwise go unrecorded. This has resulted in two themed collections of short memoir *Tangled Roots*, about mixed race families and *Who Are We Now?* on individual experiences of the Brexit Referendum. In 2019, her work was published as part of the anthology Common People (Unbound) edited by Kit De Waal. She is writing a novel set in Leeds between the 1950s and the 1970s and lives in East Sussex.